THE WAY

OF

WOMAN

DOUBLEDAY

NEW YORK LONDON TORONTO

SYDNEY AUCKLAND

THE WAY

OF

WOMAN

AWAKENING THE
PERENNIAL FEMININE

HELEN M. LUKE

PUBLISHED BY DOUBLEDAY
a division of Bantam Doubleday Dell Publishing Group, Inc.
1540 Broadway, New York, New York 10036

DOUBLEDAY and the portrayal of an anchor with a
dolphin are trademarks of Doubleday, a division of Bantam Doubleday
Dell Publishing Group, Inc.

"The Bridge of Humility," "The Perennial Feminine," "The Sense of Humor," "Mother and Daughter Mysteries," and "Letting Go" originally appeared in *PARABOLA* magazine. Used with permission.

"A Freedom to Be Oneself" originally appeared in *Anima*. Used with permission.

"Inner Relationship and Community," "Suffering," "Levels," "The Cat Archetype," "The Inner Story," "An African Tale," and "The Marriage Vow" originally appeared in *Kaleidoscope*, Parabola Books, 1992. Used with permission.

"The Life of the Spirit in Women," "Mother and Daughter Mysteries," "Straw and Gold," and "Money and the Feminine Principle of Relatedness" originally appeared in *Woman: Earth and Spirit, The Feminine in Symbol and Myth*, copyright © 1981 by Helen M. Luke. Reprinted by permission of the CROSSROAD Publishing Co., New York.

"Eowyn" and "Orual" originally appeared in an Apple Farm pamphlet entitled "The Way of Woman: Ancient and Modern." Used with permission.

Charles Williams, *Taliessen through Logres*. London: Oxford University Press, 1954. Used with permission.

Library of Congress Cataloging-in-Publication Data
Luke, Helen M., 1904–
The way of woman : awakening the perennial feminine / Helen M. Luke.
p.   cm.
1. Women—Religious life.   2. Spirituality.   I. Title.
BL625.7.L85   1995
291.4′082—dc20   95-15929
                                                             CIP

Book design by Claire Naylon Vaccaro

CONTENTS

CONTENTS

PART III

PART IV

FOREWORD

A condition of complete simplicity
(Costing not less than everything)

T. S. ELIOT, "LITTLE GIDDING"

Although I never met her, Helen Luke has been a companion and guide on my journey to consciousness. Twenty years ago, as a student at the C. G. Jung Institute in Switzerland, I found myself looking for words to express some deep yearning that I could not quite fathom. Dream images were not being fully assimilated because, at the still point of knowing, they were escaping me. Then one night I came upon "The Perennial Feminine." As I read, I could feel my blood pounding through my body. "Yes, yes, yes," I kept saying. "Yea, Helen whoever-you-are. Right on!"

Leafing through this old Xerox copy which I have repeatedly pulled out of my files over the years, I laugh as I realize it is almost totally underlined with different colors of ink. As my comprehension grew, I understood at different levels, and different phrases were charged with new meaning. The gift Helen Luke gave to me was her mirroring of my feeling function—the validation of my feminine values. Others had validated my intellectual and intuitive perceptions; others had guided my descent into my shadow. Helen Luke said to me, "You are a woman. I am a woman. I know how hard it is to stand for the feminine values in a patriarchal society. Do not betray your reality." And the reality she articulated was the reality I was just beginning to live.

Reading Helen Luke is like sitting by a pool and watching a water lily unfold. Sitting in the silence, we muse on the great stem that sways as the water is kissed by the breeze. On the strength of the root that holds firm however the waters are hurled. And as we muse, one petal unfolds. And perhaps the next day another, until one day the whole blossom has unfolded to the sun. Creation opening herself to consciousness.

The power of Helen Luke's writing is in its simplicity. Only a person who has lived the tension of the opposites, who has been strong enough to hold the still point until the unity beyond the opposites becomes manifest, could articulate so clearly. Like Horowitz playing Scriabin, she has distilled the contradictions of life into its paradoxes and dances that essence in her writing.

And, like Horowitz, she can strike one note with one finger with such sensitivity that it resonates forever in our soul. Take, for example, "Only the images by which we live can bring transformation" ("The Perennial Feminine"). The statement is self-evident. Yet most of us need to remind ourselves every day that there are no microwave ovens in the royal kitchens. We cannot digest gobbled food, nor can we digest gobbled images. Both food and images that we can chew, digest, and assimilate are essential in our transformations toward wholeness. Helen's prose is woven in images, both those that were natively her own from her dreams, and those she made her own from literature—the Bible, Dante, Shakespeare, Eliot.

Striking that one note is equally evident in her psychological clarity. In her interview entitled "The Only Freedom" she was asked, "Is the shadow a kind of mirror?" "Oh, very much so. It is the mirror of the opposite within you," she replied. In that response lies her whole understanding of the objectivity that can lead to freedom. The layers of meaning in that thought can resonate even into old age.

I am honored to write this Foreword. On behalf of countless women and men, I say, "Thank you, Helen. Thank you for guiding me to the courage of my own feminine depths. Thank you for strengthening me in finding my feminine voice. Thank you for steadfastly living the feminine values in a society that, consciously and unconsciously, despises them. Thank you for encouraging me to go where I might never have dared to go alone. And thank you for shining the light into corridors where I have yet to go."

Even as I write, the flame of Helen Luke's life is flickering ever more faintly in this earthly reality and even more brightly in the eternal Now. Thank you, Helen, for the legacy you so joyously pass on to us—your passion to celebrate the feminine, the masculine, and their divine union within.

Marion Woodman
January 5, 1995

THE WAY

OF

WOMAN

INTRODUCTION

When Helen Luke's ninetieth birthday was celebrated on October 15, 1994, the primary tribute to Helen was a reading of Sophocles's *Oedipus at Colonos*, a classic tragedy about the death of an aged king written by the poet when he himself was in his nineties. Moved by the drama and by the occasion, Helen responded by telling a story that she herself had just read, one that spoke eloquently to her about the spiritual needs of our world today.

The story had originally been told to the Sufi poet Rumi by his master Shams-i-Tabriz. Rumi in turn had told the story as a part of his *Discourses*. As Helen in turn told the story:

> *A caravan of men and camels crossed a desert and reached a place where they expected to find water. Instead they found only a hole going deep into the earth. They lowered bucket after bucket into the hole, but the rope each time came back empty—no bucket and no water. They then began to lower men into the hole, but the men, too, disappeared off the end of the rope. Finally a wise man among the party volunteered to go down into the hole in search of water.*
>
> *When the wise man reached the bottom of the hole, he found himself face to face with a horrible monster. The wise man thought to himself,*

*"I can't hope to escape from this place, but I can at least remain aware
of everything I am experiencing." The monster said to him, "I will let
you go only if you answer my question." He answered, "Ask your
question."*

The monster said, "Where is the best place to be?"

*The wise man thought to himself, "I don't want to hurt his feelings.
If I name some beautiful city, he may think I'm disparaging his home-
town. Or maybe this hole is the place he thinks is best." So to the
monster he said, "The best place to be is wherever you feel at home—
even if it's a hole in the ground."*

*The monster said, "You are so wise that I will not only let you go,
but I will also free the foolish men who came down before you. And I
will release the water in this well."*

Helen found considerable power in this story, returning to it again
and again in conversation during the weeks between her birthday and
her death on January 6, 1995. She intended to use Rumi's story—or "The
Story of the Monster," as she more often called it—as the core of the
Introduction to the present book. From the beginning, story was the
vehicle through which Helen spoke, not so much creating stories as
responding to them at a very deep level and sharing that response with
others. Dante's *Commedia*, Homer's *Odyssey*, Shakespeare's *The Tempest*,
the novels of Charles Williams, African tales, all called from her the
profound reflections that comprise the bulk of her writing.

In introducing Helen's 1987 *Old Age*, I wrote that "in Helen Luke's
writings, the great images that she finds for us are in familiar literary
texts, though the images need her special perceptiveness to reveal their
meanings to us." We no longer have access to that "special perceptiveness," and thus will never know all that her extraordinary mind would
have revealed about the meanings of Rumi's story. We do know, though,
that it spoke to her as *the* story for our time and that it was for her the
appropriate introduction to this collection. It is thus worth our hazarding
a few speculations about its meanings in the light of her earlier writing
and of her comments to others about the story.

"The true story," she once wrote, "springs out of the archetypal patterns underlying all human life, the perennial battle between good and evil. . . . Even in the simplest and most primitive of traditional fairy stories, it is human choice that decides the issue." And in such great tragic stories as those of Shakespeare, "we are swept into the overwhelming terror of archetypal forces as they seize upon human beings and transform them, dragging them either into Hell or, with individual choice, through Hell to Heaven." The key words here are "individual choice." In "Rumi's Story," the attraction for Helen seemed to lie, first of all, in the individual choices made by the wise-man hero. He chose to go down into the darkness in search of the water of life; even more important, he chose to remain aware of what he was experiencing rather than closing his eyes to the terrors of darkness and monstrosity. Such choices echo Helen's own intense awareness, first, of the darkness at the heart of the mystery and of the immense darkness of our own time and, second, of the pressing need for the wise man and woman to seek for the water of life deep in the darkness and to remain open-eyed in the face of the monstrous.

The significance of the hero's choosing to go down into the earth is indirectly commented upon in Helen's essay, "The Lord's Prayer," where, in discussing the phrase "Thy will be done in earth," she insists on what she calls "the old form of the words 'in earth' ":

> The seed of the creative must descend into the earth, not on top of the earth, and be hidden in her womb . . . in order that the kingdom . . . may be born, the Will be done, and the awareness of . . . the dance of creation may awaken in man. . . . [At] all times we must affirm [the Creator's] transcendence, but it is wholly meaningless if we stand gazing upward, trying to lift our feet off the earth and identifying with a nebulous goodness dwelling ever in the light with no darkness to cloud it. . . . Only in the darkness of the earth can the Kingdom be real to us.

As we know from her other writings, if one descends into the darkness —especially the darkness of the unconscious—one must go in full awareness and must remain aware. Otherwise one ends up like those the monster called "the foolish men"; one remains, that is, trapped in the dark cave with the monster. As she once wrote about the blind search for the mystery within, about "short cuts to the inner vision": "The danger can be very great, for the unconscious can swallow as well as nourish, and the Spirit from within, seized upon by the immature ego, becomes a demon overthrowing all human values. . . . Then indeed the end is a descent from the superhuman to the subhuman."

Central then are the hero's choices to descend and to remain fully aware. But we know from Helen's comments to friends that Rumi's story spoke to her about more than just these courageous choices. She mentioned again and again the hero's courtesy toward, and his respect for, the terrible creature at the bottom of the well. She shared with C. G. Jung an awareness of the great darkness within and without and the necessity for the individual to face that darkness with courage. Her attraction to Rumi's story suggests that, in her last weeks, she was focusing on our need to face that darkness with courtesy and respect as well. Jung wrote (in a letter that Helen delighted in quoting) of seeing "even in the blackest night . . . a great light" and of sensing "great kindness in the abysmal darkness." Jung's reference was to the darkness of the deity. But one wonders if Helen's intense response indicates that Rumi's story suggested to her that our own choice to show compassion and courtesy to whatever we find in the abysmal darkness might be what releases that great kindness. One of Helen's own stories—a blend of dream and active imagination—suggests the validity of this reading of the wise man's courtesy. In Helen's story the dreamer enters the earth in a series of continuing descents until she, too, faces a monster even more horrible than that faced by Rumi's wise man; her courteous response to the monster causes the monster's talons to tear into its own horrid entrails instead of into the dreamer's eyes. As in Rumi's story, not only is the dreamer freed from the darkness and the monster, but the dreamer's action of speaking courteously releases a gift for the world—in Helen's story, in the form of the golden hair into which the dying monster is transformed and which the dreamer brings back up into the daylight world.

Surely it is not incidental that the wise man's action in Rumi's story leads to a freeing of the trapped men and a releasing of the life-giving water. All who know Helen's words know how fervently she agreed with

Jung that no less than the fate of the world depends on the spiritual progress of the individual. She quoted often and with great feeling Jung's words (from "The Undiscovered Self") about the "mood of universal destruction and renewal that has set its mark on our age" and Jung's questions about the world's future:

> So much is at stake and so much depends on the psychological constitution of modern man. Is he conscious of the path he is treading, and what the conclusions are that must be drawn from the present world situation and his own psychic situation? Does he know that he is on the point of losing the life-preserving myth of the inner man which Christianity has treasured up for him? Does he realize what lies in store should this catastrophe ever befall him? Is he even capable of realizing that this would in fact be a catastrophe? And, finally, does the individual know that he is the makeweight that tips the scales?

It was this final question to which Helen returned again and again in her own counseling. She also quoted Jung's statement that "one does not become enlightened by imagining figures of light but by making the darkness conscious." This seems in part what happens in that dark space where the wise man meets the monster and becomes the makeweight that tips the scales as, through his awareness and his courtesy, he sets free his companions and releases the water.

Rumi's story stands in interesting conjunction with the "African Tale" included in this volume, a story that Helen told in her address to a class of women on their graduation from St. Mary's College. "An African Tale," too, is about going down into the darkness—though there it was the darkness of a lake or river rather than the earth. It, too, is about courtesy and compassion, as the young girl obeys the old woman's injunction to lick her sores and is rewarded by being protected from the monster and by being given a wonderful necklace. One can learn a great deal about Helen's reading of a story by her responses to the details of this African tale, a story that seems (and that Helen obviously felt to be) appropriate for those setting out on the journey. Rumi's story is perhaps more in keeping with the later parts of our journey. Whatever the monster we face in the darkness—our own shadow, the darkness of our world today, the darkness at the heart of the mystery—we face it more or less alone, with our eyes open, only hoping that the courtesy and good will we bring to the encounter will save us and somehow mysteriously set free others and release the water we all need in order to live.

To think deeply about Rumi's story, knowing how central it was for Helen as she approached her own death, makes us wish with even more longing for Helen herself—for that profound insight she brought to such stories and to their place in our lives. It also makes us most grateful for the writings that she did leave us, some of the most important of which are contained in the pages of this book. For these writings, and for her life, we would say, with Marion Woodman, "Thank you, Helen."

Barbara Adams Mowat

PART

I

THE BRIDGE OF
HUMILITY

What is that forever elusive yet longed-for thing, humility? It is the one quality that, if one could ever think of oneself as possessing it, would in that instant be lost. Perhaps the very longing for it—for the safety of it—is proof that it is not there. What greater pride could there be than the ego's boast, "I have found humility!"

The word comes from *humus*, the soil. It is the quality of the soil, the passive earth, the "dirt" in American parlance, from which all things grow. The feminine soil—if only one could be just that—passive, quiet, receiving the seed, waiting for the sun to shine, for the rain to fall from Heaven—quite without responsibility for anything. What a rest that would be from all foolish striving. Would one not simply be humble then, identified with the *humus*, the soil of life? But humility, alas! is not *humus* —it is not a quality of nature but of man.

Even the simplest woman cannot remain simply "herself," pure female, if she is not to lose that most vital of all her qualities—her humanity. She cannot abdicate from the responsibility of consciousness, however rudimentary, and it is a responsibility which demands that she, no less than man, her brother, must never "cease from exploration" (T. S. Eliot, "Little Gidding") until she finds within her own being the sower of the seed, the creator of the light, as well as the passive earth; and all the time both man and woman are inevitably held in never ending tension between hubris ("I am the sun") and inertia ("I am the helpless victim") which can so easily be disguised behind the self-satisfied masks of good works or of resignation.

Only humility can release us from this tension. Could it be defined as the final realization that all creation is feminine to God in the "heavens" of the spirit? The sun as well as the soil? As long as one yearns to be only the one or only the other, there is no creation, no marriage of human and divine, no child and no humility.

For instance, as I lay still and relaxed, and suddenly these thoughts and images began dropping into my mind, I felt a spurious peace. I was *humus*, the soil. But the real peace lies beyond thought and image, and it can only come—as I have learned over many years—after I have fought the inertia of my feminine passivity—after I have obeyed the demand from the core of my being and made the often agonizing effort to put into words the emerging thoughts. Why? Says my spurious humility, Why do you have to do this? You'll probably only wreck their spontaneity with your clumsy expression and you only do it so as to get approval. And anyway, there is nothing important about preserving them.

For another the imperative may be to paint or build or to form the passive image in any one of a thousand ways. For me and for many women, it is the discipline of the word. The point is that one must make incarnate in some form or other both the active sun and the passive earth of being. And one day, instead of leaping from one to the other, the two together will become "feminine to God," in humility.

As I lay writing these things, the facile dozing of old age took over for brief minutes and, as ever, I was aware of seemingly incoherent images of all sorts just over the edge of consciousness, and I felt again the fear of fragmentation. And then came the image of that most fascinating of toys —the kaleidoscope, and I saw all those tiny bits of colored glass jumbled together meaninglessly until I looked through the glass at the end of the tube and saw them in beautiful mandala patterns through the process of "reflection." "Reflection"—a bending again—a looking anew from a different angle. The word "kaleidoscope" is made up of *kalos*, beautiful; and *eidos*, form; and *scope*, outlook or view. Our view for most of the time of all the little colored chips of life is meaningless, has no form, but if we could only "reflect" thus, rebend them, then we should see the beautiful form in them with the eye of the Godhead in whom they are whole, and we should recognize at once the great mandala pattern in which the ego's hubris and inertia disappear.

Meanwhile, the reflecting, the rebending in search of the beautiful form, must be worked at consciously little by little, again and again, without pride in achievement, without despair in failure. Indeed, then, out of our sight the seed may sprout, the flower may be drawn upward to the light of the sun, and the roots may reach down into the soil to the waters under the earth; and then at last water, sun, soil, seed and flower and the fruit of human consciousness itself—all become the *humus* of God; and so humility can be born.

In his novel *The Place of the Lion*, Charles Williams wrote:

No mind was so good that it did not need another mind to counter and equal it, and to save it from conceit and blindness and bigotry and folly. Only in such a balance could humility be found, humility which was a lucid speed to welcome lucidity whenever and wherever it presented itself. How much he owed to Quentin! How much—not pride but delight urged the admission—Quentin owed to him! Balance—and movement in balance, as an eagle sails up on the wind—this was the truth of life, and beauty in life.

THE PERENNIAL
FEMININE

The women's movements of this century have brought many splendid changes and have given to the lives of millions of women a freedom rarely dreamed of a hundred years ago. But, as always, such rapid changes bring with them great dangers which can become the roots of evils which remain unrecognized and are therefore projected onto convenient "enemies" such as man. It is therefore vital, if the new freedoms are to become real in our lives, that individual women recognize the necessity of connecting the theories expounded and the emotions aroused in her with the symbolic life of her feminine psyche. Without this inner work, however things may appear on the surface, the new freedoms may turn to dark and destructive conflicts in her soul.

Where, however, is a woman to look for nourishment for her inner imagery as her new personality struggles for birth? The changes in the way of Eve have come with staggering swiftness, but it seems to me that only recently has the realization broken through that a deeper awareness of the nature of these changes is now essential. If we are to stop the wreckage caused by the disorientation of women, by their loss of identity under the stresses of the new way, then the numinous meaning of the great challenge they face must break through from the unconscious; for no amount of rational analysis can bring healing. Only so can the images of the masculine and feminine, which have become more and more dangerously mixed in our society, be discriminated once more, so that they may come to a new synthesis in both woman and man.

It is important that we attempt to arrive at some degree of clarity about various attitudes and assumptions which are currently prevalent when people talk about woman. Those who assert that the only difference between men and women is biological, and that in every other way they are equal and have the same inborn potentialities, have disastrously missed the point. Equality of value between individuals is an eternal truth, beyond all comparisons, whereas "superior" and "inferior" are relative terms defining abilities or degrees of consciousness. Equality of opportunity for women has indeed to be fought for, but equality of value can never be understood until we have learned to discriminate and accept *difference*. The biological difference between man and woman is never a "nothing but"; it is a fundamental difference, and it does not stop with the body but implies an equally fundamental difference of *psychic* nature. No matter how consciously we may develop the contrasexual principle within us, no matter how strong our intuition of the ultimate union between the masculine and feminine elements in each individual, as long as we remain in our bodies here in space and time, we are predominantly either male or female, and we forget this at our peril. Disaster awaits a woman who imitates man, but even a woman who aims at becoming half man, half woman, and imagines she is thereby achieving archetypal "androgyny" will certainly be inferior on both counts. A woman is born to be essentially and wholly a woman and the more deeply and consciously she is able to know and live the spirit, the Logos, within her the more surely she will realize this truth. One of the most frightening characteristics of our present *Zeitgeist* is the urge to destroy difference, to reduce everything to a horrible sameness in the cause of "equality."

Whether a woman is efficient or brilliant in some sphere hitherto deemed masculine, or whether she remains in a traditionally feminine role, modern woman must discriminate and relate to the image of the masculine spirit within her, while at the same time maintaining her roots in her basic feminine nature—that which receives, nourishes, and gives birth on all levels of being through her awareness of the earth and her ability to bring up the water of life from under the earth. All her true creativeness in every aspect of her life, private or public, springs from this.

As we look back on the extremely rapid emergence of women in this century into the masculine world of thought and action, it is not surprising that woman has fallen into increased contempt for her own values. It has surely been a necessary phase, but its effects have been devastating not only on woman herself but also on the men around her. For the animus—the unconscious masculinity in a woman—when it takes possession of her femininity, has a terrifying power, charged as it is with the numinosity of the unconscious—and most men in their turn, when faced with this power in their women, either retreat into an inferior passive femininity, seeking to propitiate the power of the animus, or else react with brutal aggressive masculinity. Small wonder that women thus possessed, having lost their true roots in nature, are constantly beset by the anxious feeling of being useless, however outwardly successful. The dreams of modern women are full of this basic insecurity.

It is time for woman to turn from this hidden contempt for the feminine values so that she may cease to identify creativity solely with the productions of thought and with achievements in the outer world. It is exceedingly hard for us to realize, in the climate of Western society, that the woman who quietly *responds* with intense interest and love to people, to ideas, and to things is as deeply and truly creative as one who always seeks to lead, to act, to achieve. The feminine qualities of receptivity, of nurturing in silence and secrecy, are (whether in man or woman) as essential to creation as their masculine opposites and in no way inferior.

But these are all rational thoughts *about* the situation. What of the images without which, as I said at the outset, no change is possible? How is a woman, when she feels the immense fascination of the power of the spirit stirring in her, to welcome it and yet remain true to her womanhood, or how is she to rediscover her femininity if she has lost it? How is a man to realize the values of the heart without losing the bright sword of his spirit in the fogs of emotion? There are no intellectual answers.

Only the images by which we live can bring transformation. The future hangs on this quest for the heart of love by both sexes.

Each of us has a well of images within, which are the saving reality and from which may be born the individual myth carrying the meaning of a life. That new images are now emerging in the tales and poetry of our time is now beyond doubt. But any truly valid "new myth" cannot be rationally invented. It must be born out of the crucible of our own struggles and suffering as we affirm our new freedom without rejecting the perennial truth of the feminine way.

THE LIFE OF THE
SPIRIT IN WOMEN

THE SPIRIT AND THE ANIMUS

What is meant by the word "spirit"? There are a thousand answers, but the true meaning is glimpsed by us only through the kind of experience that can never be rationally explained in words. Only the images which perennially emerge from the unconscious of humankind may convey in a symbol the power of the spirit.

The most universal of all the images of the spirit is the breath, the wind—the *pneuma* in Greek, the *ruach* in Hebrew; it is that which "bloweth where it listeth and no man knoweth whence it cometh and whither it goeth." Closely related to this is the image of fire. Out of the wind came fire, the ancients believed. At Pentecost there came a rushing mighty wind and tongues of fire burned on each individual apostle. This wind, this fire of the spirit, must enter into a man or a woman before he or she can in truth be said to *create* anything at all. Thoughts and actions that remain untouched by this mystery may produce new forms in abundance, bringing good and evil in equal measure to our collective life, but nothing is essentially changed in the psyche of man, whereas, whenever a breath of that wind or a spark of that fire lodges in mind or heart or body, we are immediately aware of some kind of newness of life.

If we look briefly at the various contexts in which the word "spirit" occurs, from chemistry to the Christian Trinity, we see that it is predominantly used on every level and without any moral connotation to express that which brings about a transformation. Oil is transformed into power through the spirit in petroleum; spirits of salt and spirits of ammonia burn and cleanse, purify and destroy; the spirit in alcohol lifts a man out of his ego and alters his personality before our eyes; angels or demons have always been invoked to work transformations for good or evil; the spirit that emerged at Pentecost ran like fire through the pagan world and gave birth to the new Christian Era. And, greatest symbol of all, the Holy Spirit in the Godhead entered into a woman and transformed God himself into incarnate man. It is obvious from all this that the spirit basically manifests itself to Western man as an active principle, and therefore it has usually been associated with masculine creative power, though its feminine aspect has been known as Sophia, coexistent with God before creation.

Certainly it is fundamentally androgynous. But for most of us, having emerged to some degree from the original identity of archetypal opposites and being still far indeed from their conscious reunion, the paramount need is for discrimination between them. For until they are fully experienced as separate, they cannot unite in a holy marriage any more than two married people can achieve a conscious relationship until they know themselves as psychically separate. Therefore for the moment let us call the spirit *he* in accordance with our tradition.

One of the loudest complaints of the liberators of women has been that the dominance of the male in society has prevented women from proving that they are as creative as men. This is a half-truth, whereby the real truth of the matter is obscured and lost. The first essential, surely, in thinking about the transforming power of the spirit is to remember that it creates nothing in a vacuum. There has to be fuel before the fire will burn; there has to be earth as well as seed before new life is created. The masculinity of the spirit is meaningless unless it enters into a feminine container, and ultimately no man can create anything without the equal participation of the woman without or the woman within. Even God could not transform himself into man without the free consent of Mary. In every creative act or transformation—intellectual, emotional, or phys-ical—the male and the female, the active and the passive, are of equal importance, and real liberation from the weight of the inferior status imposed on women lies not in the reiterated assertion that women must now strive to live like men, but in the affirmation, so difficult for us, of the *equal value* of the specifically feminine. Nothing demonstrates more clearly the real damage which has been done to us by the dominance of masculinity for so many centuries as the contempt for the feminine implicit in so much of the propaganda of the women's movements. It even creeps unrecognized into the work of some of the most far-seeing women writers of today. Indeed, it requires a great effort of consciousness in every individual woman to remain aware of this destructive spirit which is constantly whispering to her the collective judgment of centuries about the inferiority, the dullness, the uncreativeness of her passive feminine nature. Modern woman must therefore face the great danger of assuming that she has only to throw off the *yoke* imposed on her by men and develop her *spiritual* gifts in the spheres of activity now opened to her, in order to arrive at that far-off goal of androgynous being.

The great contribution of C. G. Jung toward the restoration of feminine values to Western man is often obscured by a misunderstanding of his concept of the *animus*. In Jung's terminology the animus is a personification of the *unconscious* masculinity in women, the anima being the parallel image of the feminine in a man. Being unconscious, it is necessarily projected and often manifests itself in negative ways, and this has been interpreted entirely out of context by many of those who are devoted to the cause of liberation. Jung, they say, denies to woman any equality with man. He accuses her of producing secondhand opinions and engaging in all manner of inferior masculine activity, as though she were by nature incapable of real creativity. Nothing could be further from the truth. What Jung does affirm is that the creative power in a woman can never come to fruition if she is caught in an unconscious imitation of men or identification with the inferior masculinity in her unconscious. He defined the masculine as the ability to know one's goal and to do what is necessary to achieve it. As long as the animus remains *unconscious* in a woman, he will persuade her that she has no need to explore her hidden motives and will urge her to a blind pursuit of her conscious goals, which, of course, liberates her from the hard and undramatic task of discovering her real individual point of view. Unrecognized and undifferentiated, he will actually destroy in her the possibility of integrating her contrasexual powers. Her spirituality will thus remain a sterile thing and this negative animus will poison her attitude to her own nature. The true function of the animus is to act as an inner guide between the ego and the deep springs both of the spirit and of true feminine wisdom so that the woman may bring to birth a new consciousness of both. It is when he operates *between* her and the outer world, and she identifies with him, that he destroys her creativity. Esther Harding quoted Jung as saying in conversation that the true feminineness of the man is *not* the anima; likewise the true masculine spirit in a woman is *not* the animus, though he leads her to it. The conscious integration of her dormant spirit of clear discrimination alone can free the individual woman from the compulsive yoke of the negative animus. Without this freedom, no amount of liberation in the outer world can do more than throw her into another and more dangerous slavery.

The spiritual life is generally understood to mean the interior awareness which leads humanity into relationship to God, the Creator. The danger of mistaking an experience of spirits for the experience of the Spirit has always been recognized by the wise. "It is not every spirit, my dear people, that you can trust; test them, to see if they come from God" (Jerusalem Bible, 1 John 4:1). But this danger is greatly magnified in a time such as ours when every kind of experimentation is encouraged and promoted. It threatens a far greater number of people who are incapable of discrimination and who, since they have been largely deprived of the rituals and collective symbols by which their souls were unconsciously nourished, seek everywhere to rediscover a numinous sense of meaning in life. Charismatic movements, and mystical or occult teachings of all kinds, spring up to meet the need of thousands who have lost contact with the spiritual in the deserts of materialistic rationalism. Groups come together to induce contact with what is all too easily called the Holy Spirit. Often there is simply an opening up of the unconscious which releases an experience of the numinous. Whether or not such an experience leads to a real glimpse of the transforming power of the spirit depends on the degree of awareness in the individual and on the objectivity and humility with which she brings her vision to incarnation in her life on this earth. For the most part, these induced experiences are at once seized upon by that ambivalent pair—the anima and the animus—and the transformation remains on the level of the emotions or the will to power in the ego. People are then possessed by a hubris which heralds catastrophe.

How then are we to test the spirits? An illumination comes when we realize the extraordinary rightness of the name *Holy* Spirit—the spirit of the *whole*. The writer of the epistle of John, exhorting his readers to test the spirits, went on, "You can tell the spirits that come from God by this: every spirit which acknowledges that Jesus the Christ has come in the flesh is from God" (Jerusalem Bible, 1 John 4:2). In modern psychological language this is to say that we are justified in speaking of the spirit of God only when it leads to an incarnation in us, however small, of the spirit of truth within. This is the spirit that speaks through the *daimon* of each man or woman, calling the individual to the fulfillment of his or her unique task. On the other hand, if, when the emotion of a numinous experience is spent and the darkness returns, we simply fall from exaltation to depression; or, worse, if we find ourselves so inflated by it that we at once set out to convert others, we may be sure that we are simply possessed by the *spirits* of the undifferentiated opposites in the unconscious. The true experience is always a sacrifice of the ego's one-sidedness; it is a reception of the creative seed into the vessel of the feminine, whether in man or in woman, and usually the beginning of a long nurturing, a patient waiting for the hidden birth. "Be it unto me according to thy word."

WOMAN AND THE EARTH

It follows from the preceding reflections that, before a woman can safely pursue her goals with the true masculine discrimination that will bring her to maturity, she must first learn to recognize and to value the nature of the principle which is dominant in her by the fact of her sex. I am not denying the obvious truth that there is a great difference in the balance of the male and female elements in each person, but, whether the difference is great or small, nature tips the scale at our conception one way or the other, and no growth or transformation is ever possible until we have accepted the facts.

In innumerable counseling situations the tragic alienation of women from their femininity becomes clear. Very often the first extremely difficult task for the modern woman is to recognize her conscious and unconscious delusions about the nature of womanhood, so that she may begin to realize the extent to which her secondhand thinking is in collusion with her repressed shadow qualities, directing her behavior and even possessing her soul. This alienation must bring with it a sense of deep guilt, since it is a betrayal of one's own birthright, and this guilt is felt in all the wrong contexts and is sometimes accompanied by a sentimental religiosity in which the spirit of Christianity is lost indeed. The neuroses which result are often the saving grace because of the suffering they bring; they are a true operation of the spirit striving to awaken the woman to her predicament.

Often such a woman will reveal at once that her concepts of what it means to be a woman are concocted from notions of frivolous, empty-headed pleasure seekers pursuing sexual goals, plus an image of the dependent drudge condemned to sweeping floors or to a boring twenty-four-hour-a-day care of children. Half consciously it all adds up to a choice between whoredom and slavery, though she may not define it in this way. The first she despises, the second she fears, or vice versa, and thus she is miserably caught in an interpretation of womanhood as a choice between using men or being used by them. Yet the instinct of the feminine is precisely to *use* nothing, but simply to give and to receive. This is the nature of the earth—to receive the seed and to nourish the roots—to foster growth in the dark so that it may reach up to the light.

How are women to recover their reverence for and their joy in this great archetype of which the symbols have always been the earth, the moon, the dark, and the ocean, mother of all? For thousands of years the necessity of freeing consciousness from the grip of the destructive inertia and from the devouring quality, which are the negative side of the life-giving mother, rightly gave to the emerging spirit of activity and exploration an enormous predominance; but the extremes of this worship of the bright light of the sun have produced in our time an estrangement even in women themselves from the patient nurturing and enduring qualities of the earth, from the reflected beauty of the silver light of the moon in the darkness, from the unknown in the deep sea of the unconscious and from the springs of the water of life. The way back and down to those springs and to the roots of the tree is likewise the way on and up to the spirit of air and fire in the vaults of heaven.

If we read the second sign of the *I Ching*, K'un the Receptive, which describes the yin, the feminine principle, the equal and opposite of yang the creative, we shall find beautifully expressed there the essence of these things:

> *The Earth's condition is receptive devotion.*
> *Perfect indeed is the sublimity of the Receptive.*
> *All beings owe their birth to it because it*
> *receives the heavenly with devotion.*
> *. . . Seek not works but bring to completion . . .*
> *To hide beauty does not mean to be inactive.*
> *It means only that beauty must not be displayed*
> *at the wrong time.*

The Receptive does not lead but follows, since it is like a vessel in which the light is hidden until it can appear *at the right time*. Thus it has no need for a willed purpose or for the prestige of recognized achievement.

Two warnings are added—the first is against the danger of inertia: "When there is a hoarfrost underfoot, solid ice is not far off." The second speaks of the destructive results when the passive value takes the lead and *opposes* the active forces of yang. It then produces real evil if held to. It may simply swallow up any new growth of consciousness.

If we can rediscover in ourselves the hidden beauty of this receptive devotion, if we can learn how to be still without inaction, how to "further life" without willed purpose, how to serve without demanding prestige, and how to nourish without domination: then we shall be women again out of whose earth the light may shine.

THE ACADEMIC WOMAN

A friend confided to me the other day that she still suffered from guilty feelings because she felt incapable of producing *original* thoughts. These feelings came to her, she said, especially at moments when she had read a book of great creative originality to which she had felt an immediate response. She would ask herself why she was always able to follow but not initiate. Very few women who have grown up in this century are free from this brand of guilt complex in one form or another. To those of clear mind and differentiated feeling, it may come in the manner expressed by my friend. In a great many others the guilt produces a positively compulsive desire to go to school—to acquire academic degrees—to own pieces of paper with printed evidence of achievements which will, they believe, prove at last that they are people of worth. As long as the degrees are necessary for a person's work or for a stimulus to expansion of the mind, it is well and good; but the drive often has little or no relationship either to practical necessity or to a genuine love of learning. It is found not only in those who have been deprived of opportunities for university education but frequently also in the well-educated and intellectually brilliant. It is a drive far more damaging to women than to men and much more often found in them because, although a man may feel cheated of opportunities if he has not been to college, his sense of worth as a person rarely depends upon it. But the acquisition of mental and rational skills appears to innumerable modern women as the only way to escape the sense of inferiority that besets them.

A highly intelligent and able woman told me that her fear of not achieving a doctorate was driving her into a state of neurotic anxiety which was affecting her whole life. She had a good marriage, children, a teaching job which she enjoyed and did well and for which a doctorate was in no way necessary. Yet because the prestige attached to it seemed to her the only thing that could give her any real assurance of her worth, she was pouring a huge amount of her vital energy into research for her thesis. She could have explored her chosen subject without pressure and for the joy of it, once the desperate need for academic status was removed, but because of this imagined need the joy was, of course, lost. The anxiety thus generated, and the ever growing resistance from the unconscious which made it harder and harder for her to write anything, was affecting her health and her relationships with family, colleagues, and friends, and worst of all, it was progressively cutting off the springs of her sense of meaning in the unconscious. She had no time outwardly and no energy inwardly to be still and listen. Thus the earth and the water of womanhood in such a person is scorched and dried up by the destructive forces of fire and air. This may sound like an extraordinary and exaggerated state of affairs: on the contrary, it is very common among women with unusual thinking abilities.

The onset of severe neurosis in a woman of this quality of mind usually occurs, in my experience, when she is approaching the mid-point of life, and when she has already achieved considerable success in her profession. I knew one such woman who was a fine scholar and was also highly thought of as a teacher by both faculty and students. She had a good marriage and two young children; and to all who knew her superficially it would seem that the gods had indeed blessed her with every ingredient for a full and balanced life in which both her feminine eros and her masculine logos qualities could blossom. Yet when I first knew her she was suffering from neurotic symptoms so severe that her job was threatened and her children were obviously disturbed. She was subject to attacks of dizziness that would come upon her in the middle of her classes or while driving her car, and she struggled on with great courage as her fear increased. She began to explore the images in her unconscious, and she soon recognized the recurring theme through dream after dream in which she sought desperately to establish a sense of identity and meaning in her life through the prestige of mental activity acceptable to examiners or academic gatherings of men. It also became very clear that what she was really searching for was a new religious attitude to life—in short, for the inspiration of the spirit, and that this spirit had become almost wholly identified with the pseudomasculine activity of her animus.

She had in her youth been in true and living contact with the symbolic life of the Catholic Church, and through it she had been nourished inwardly. But for modern persons with a capacity for consciousness the old unconscious nourishment is not enough. If they are not to lose contact with the living water of faith and the flame of the spirit, each one must find these things individually as well as collectively through real self-knowledge and attention to her own spontaneous imagery. If an intellectually gifted woman does not set out on this path, she is apt gradually to fall prey to the negative animus who so easily disguises himself as the true Logos. Unseen and unrecognized, he takes to himself and uses as a weapon the mistrust and contempt for the feminine way which surrounds us all. My friend had succumbed to this danger, and, although when I met her she was still trying to keep the spirit alive in herself by outer allegiance to her church, her interior life was growing more and more meaningless because of her alienation from her own truth and from the mystery of being. Very well, it may be said, if what she needs is a renewal of spirituality, let her turn to some strenuous spiritual discipline or charismatic group so that she may experience the "rushing mighty wind" or the sudden flame. Or others may recommend that she undertake some creative writing in her field which will give a sense of meaning. But these things are in themselves no cure for such a condition; neither asceticism, forced meditation, short cuts to the numinous, emotional release, nor the foredoomed attempt to create out of a sterile soil can avail unless and until she finds and experiences what it means to be a woman.

As has been said, no one, either man or woman, creates anything without the cooperation of the contrasexual element, but when a woman of the kind I am describing tries to produce original work she goes at it, as it were, upside down. She starts from secondhand masculine thinking and is frustrated—even panic-stricken—when the feminine soil on which she is working refuses to come to life. And this situation extends into her whole life. She has then to learn to start from the receptive, the hidden, the goalless aspect of yin, and gradually the true light of the spirit will shine in the darkness, and the intellect too will be illumined and come to its fruition.

For a highly educated woman to learn again to trust that feminine kind of thinking, which Jung has called the natural mind, when once she has lost faith in it, is an inner quest demanding indeed the "perseverance of a mare," as the I Ching says. In Memories, Dreams, Reflections, Jung described the strange irrational appearance of the feminine natural mind in his own mother, and we feel the great importance of this in his boyhood years when he found in it nourishment for his own extraordinary early awareness of the two kinds of thinking. But once lost by the instinctive woman it is only reborn through a conscious and painful sacrifice. For my friend it took the form of a decision to resign from her fine university job for an unspecified length of time—to stay at home with her children, to dig in her garden, to apply her imagination and her powers of discrimination outwardly in her cooking and housekeeping and in observing her daily reactions to her family—and inwardly by quiet attention to the images behind her life, which had for so long been ignored.

"What a comedown!" is the almost universal reaction to such a decision in this day and age. "Dr. So-and-so is wasting her great talents on work which any ignorant person can do," and so on. The encounter with this lack of understanding brings with it the crucial experience, the cross without which there is no individuation, no rebirth into a new awareness of the meaning for which one was born.

My friend faced the misunderstandings, the hostility, the loneliness, and accepted the loss of that prestige which is the lifeblood of the negative animus. Support from a few she had. All have need of it from at least one person at such moments, and it is always there if we have courage enough to face the vital choice. Perhaps only women who have made a similar sacrifice can fully appreciate the awful feeling of the loss of all known landmarks, the sense of failure, the fear of worthlessness, that come to one who makes this choice.

I am not, of course, suggesting that all women with such a problem must make their sacrifice in this particular way. But in some form or other the break must be made—a defeat accepted—a loss of prestige endured, even if it is not recognized as such by others. I remember that Simone Weil wrote in one of her essays that an essential ingredient in the soul's journey through affliction was the experience of social rejection —and that whether this was suffered neurotically (to use our language), through projection, or in outer fact was not important so long as the resulting affliction was fully accepted and endured—in which case, of course, the projection is finally made conscious and can be withdrawn.

At this point it may be helpful to digress for a moment and look at the case of a man who had to go through a similar crisis—the similarities to the woman's predicament and the differences. In the case cited, the neurotic conflict was evident in the long-continued inability of this intelligent and deeply religious man to write his doctoral thesis. All his studies were done, his notes were completed, but the minute he sat down to write, a compulsive block took over and in agony of mind and heart he sought one escape after another. He had come at last to the final year of the permissible extensions of time; his sense of inferiority was profound and he sought by sheer will and discipline to force himself to write; in his case there was a necessity to get the doctorate if he was to keep his job in the university in which he was greatly respected as man and teacher. He could not do it. For some time it had been obvious that the resistance was not in this man a mere weakness, as he had persisted in believing, but was a true protest from the unconscious. His *daimon* simply would not allow him to proceed along the royal road of a distinguished and safe academic career. He was, in fact, a priest, and his vocation was a spiritual, not an intellectual, one. But he could not pass straight from the one to the other. Suddenly he knew that the resistance was not a weakness and recognized it at last as a voice of the spirit speaking to him like Balaam's ass, standing in the way and refusing to let his master pass along a road which for him meant disaster. It had come to him not as a clear voice from on high, but from a stubborn, donkey-like, totally irrational resistance working through the instinctive wisdom of his *feminine* unconscious. He, too, made a great choice. He resigned his job in spite of the well-meaning opposition of almost all, and for two years or more he taught small children in a remote place.

So far the essentials are the same; the intellectual life has been substituted for the spiritual in both the man and the woman, as in countless others of both sexes. The immediate sacrifice was also the same—the giving up of a job which carried great prestige and security for an unknown future. The saving resistance came also from the same source—from the rejected feminine values of feeling and from the repressed natural mind which is without the goals of the conscious will. In this man's new work his energy was released from the hopeless struggle, his feeling qualities matured, and he had time and leisure to look within and search for the dominant thought in his life. He endured his spiritual conflict and found his vocation as priest which he had almost lost in those days of academic struggle. With it his authority as a man emerged, whereas before he had been in many ways still a boy. Thereupon, without any effort on his part, the way opened for him, and all he had sacrificed was restored to him in a priestly instead of an intellectual context. His prestige returned, but he was no longer imprisoned in it or dominated by it. His spirit was set free to grow, nourished now by the earth of the feminine within him.

In the woman's case, however, the outcome was surprisingly different. Inwardly she made contact with her womanhood as he did with his masculine strength, but she also discovered that, unlike the man, she did indeed have a vocation to the academic life. A woman with that kind of talent is usually born to develop and to live it. His resistance came from the straightforward fact that he had mistaken his calling and rejected the feminine values, and hers was the voice of her spirit crying out to her that she would fail altogether in her true calling as teacher and thinker because she was trying to follow it at the expense of her womanhood, in imitation of men, instead of allowing it to grow out of the earth of her feminine nature.

She, then, had returned to her *earth* as best she could. At first she felt clumsy, inept, moving in an alien element. Yet she persevered through all her doubts and consented with *receptive devotion* to employ her animus on work that brought no sense of achievement, to the making of those childlike pictures and fantasies, called by Jung active imagination, which seem to the rational mind entirely pointless. Most of all, outwardly she was helped by a suddenly discovered love of gardening, of planting and tending growing things. It is not to be supposed that the animus accepted all this lying down; he produced emotional storms and worked on her sense of failure with renewed vigor. But these affects were not merely negative. They forced her to remember and to affirm her calling to academic life and her need for it. But first she had to endure the waiting and hide the light of her mind until the right time should come. She was in *the service of the king,* who is the Self, and who demands that we seek not works but completeness in our lives.

Thus, as in so many, the cause of the neurosis in both the man and the woman lay in their subjection to the collective contempt for the feminine way of *receptive devotion.*

Marie-Louise von Franz, in her studies of the feminine in fairy tales, points out how frequently the way of the heroine involves a considerable time of withdrawal from the world, which for us means introversion, when she must go apart and endure the suffering of silent waiting for the time of her deliverance. Then comes the moment of a mature and conscious reunion with the hero, whose quest, in contrast, has involved vigorous action.

So it is within the individual. The woman had to wait for the return of her creative spirit. The time came when she felt ready to teach again. The many anxieties surrounding the work also returned to plague her, but she faced them now with far more detachment and acceptance. Then, unsought by her, came a suggestion that she apply for a position involving administration as well as teaching, and giving scope for all her exceptional qualities of mind and personality. It was time for the new light to shine. To this woman, as in the case of the man, the new opportunity came at the exact moment of readiness. The synchronicity is impressive; always it is manifest when the spirit is truly at work.

Let it not be supposed that through any of our human transformations we are freed from our conflicts. The healing of a neurosis comes not from a removal of the conflicts that were its cause, but precisely by a realization of the reality of these conflicts and by a full and free acceptance of the suffering they bring. "All opposites are of God—therefore man must bend to their burden, and in so doing he finds that God in his 'oppositeness' has taken possession of him, incarnated himself in him. He becomes a vessel filled with divine conflict." That which used to be so laden with guilt and pettiness is filled with meaning.

When she returned to her calling and took up this new and exacting work, my friend had to face extreme pressures from outside and from her own insecurity, but she was now able to carry them by virtue of a fundamental change in her whole attitude to the receptive in life. She could now begin to "carry the outer world" and her own conflicts. Her reborn eros brought new warmth and acceptance into her relationships, and her teaching and work of leadership now sprang more and more from that response to meaning which *is* the creative gift of woman.

If women in work of an intellectual or administrative kind were to remember that their greatest contribution to this world of reason and logic comes from the feeling responses of their nature, much of the wreckage caused by personality clashes and neuroses could be averted. This does not mean that they are not to *think*. On the contrary, their thinking may well be of a particularly clear and incisive nature, because it springs from their own truth of feeling. Every good teacher knows that on her love for the subject she is teaching depends her ability to pass it on to others. Responding to her love with heart and mind together, she so recreates the subject that others in their turn may respond.

This brings us back to the comment about lack of original thinking in women. It is indeed easy for all to fall prey to this unconscious assumption that only original thoughts are worthy of being called creative, and so to lose sight of the truth that feminine originality lies in the capacity for unique individual *responses*, and that this is every bit as creative as the production of new ideas. This is the sure vocation of the majority of women; only the few are born to make new discoveries in the realm of ideas. Nothing can stop the genius of these few—Mme. Curie, for instance—but it is a real tragedy when so much is lost to the world by the efforts of finely endowed women to create in an imitative masculine way, instead of responding to the images either in themselves or in the work of others, thus bringing fruition to their own creative spirits.

Is this *creative resonance*, as Jung called it, an inferior thing? A woman is not truly liberated until she knows its supreme value with her whole self.

WOMAN IN THE ARTS

It is an obvious fact that not only in the realm of thought but also in the arts there have been very few women of towering genius in comparison with men. We do not know what the future may bring, now that equality of opportunity is increasingly real and the weight of belief in the *proper* work of woman is lifted. There is, of course, already an enormous flowering of talent among women in every sphere, but it may well be that for as long as we still live in the dimensions of time and space, where differentiation between the masculine and the feminine is the essential for consciousness, the number of women manifesting artistic and literary *genius* will remain small.

I hasten to add that this is not to say that the extraordinary influx of the spirit which we call genius comes more often to men than to women. Surely there have always been as many women as men in this rare category, but usually we do not see the feminine genius because it does not often come to expression in an art or science but is at its greatest in the sphere of relationship. Even those who are most indebted to it are sometimes quite unaware of the unseen genius in mother or wife or friend which has created the atmosphere wherein their own spirits have been nourished and set free. So the *creative reasonance of the feminine being* remains unrecognized.

It is significant that in the performing arts the achievements of women have equaled those of men. Names of superlatively great actresses, dancers, singers, come quickly to mind—Mrs. Siddons, Duse, Bernhardt, Pavlova, Jenny Lind, for example. In one branch of literature —the art of fiction—there have also been several women among the giants. But when we seek to name poets, painters, or composers, the contrast is obvious. There are a number of fine women poets, but in the *supreme* category, after naming Sappho, we pause to reflect—Emily Dickinson, Emily Brontë perhaps, and then? Almost no painters leap into memory and interestingly enough no composers at all, music being the most spiritual, the furthest from the earth, of all the arts.

Acting and dancing are in their essence arts of response and therefore peculiarly feminine. The artist becomes a vessel for the spirit of the character he or she represents, and this character is recreated by each great performer. The writing of fiction likewise depends on response, on the feeling for relationships between people and things. This kind of response is, of course, not at all the same thing as an instinctive reaction. On the contrary, only when the spirit of clear, discriminating intelligence fertilizes her responses does the woman's recreation of that which she receives from another become an act of individual genius. Christmas without a conscious response to the Annunciation is unthinkable.

The stature of an artist is rarely known in his or her own time, and anyway I am not competent to make any critical judgments. It is, however, certain that the creative spirit in woman is everywhere expressing itself in the arts with great vitality and not least in the grand art of poetry. How much of this work will emerge as lastingly great we cannot yet know. Meanwhile, the openness of all true artists to the collective forces in the unconscious always carries with it specific dangers for the ego, and I believe this to be particularly so for the creative woman when she is exposed to the collective pressures of the present almost universal demand for *publicity*. It is injurious enough to any artist, but for a woman it is a threat not only to her art but to the essence of her life.

I use the word "publicity" here in its widest meaning, not in the context of literary publication. One of the major psychological diseases today is the urge to make everything public; to keep anything hidden or secret is felt to be almost a crime. Emotions are evoked and expressed in large groups; mystical or spiritual experiences are shared with as many as possible; workshops are founded in which people work publicly on the most private things; and statistics are collected with fervor so that all manifestations of the human spirit may be documented and publicized as indisputable truth. None of this is evil in itself. The urge to share creative thoughts is an essential good, and the value of group activity and of statistics is beyond question. But the extremes, sponsored by those with genuine concern for humanity as well as by the media of our society, are largely destroying the sense of mystery itself and with it the essential value of the individual *secret*, without which a man and, still more dangerously, a woman, loses contact with the soul. The individual soul cannot grow in public, for the kingdom of heaven is within, and the prayer of the spirit is in secret. "Go to your private room and, when you have shut your door, pray to your Father who is in that secret place" (Jerusalem Bible, Matthew 6:6). As it is with prayer, so with all creative work, which is, in fact, itself a form of prayer, being an individual expression of the mystery of being. The light which is born in secret will shine out when the time is ripe and be seen perhaps by few, perhaps by many; the number is irrelevant.

Let us think of two women who were great poets and try to imagine what might have happened to them in our day. Both Emily Brontë and Emily Dickinson lived in extreme seclusion. They were withdrawn from the world; neither left home more than once or twice in the course of her life. Brontë's one novel and her few poems were among the undisputed masterpieces of the English language, but she shunned even limited publicity. Jane Austen was at great pains to preserve her anonymity. Elizabeth Jenkins says in her biography of Jane Austen, ". . . whatever the motive which led her to refuse to enter society as an authoress, she was actually obeying a profound instinct of self preservation . . . nothing would have induced her to accept a position, even in her family, in which she had to support a well-defined attitude or to be anything but the most ordinary of human beings; such a position would have been abhorrent to the conscious mind, and it would have threatened that capacity of vision that was the inspiration of her art."

Dickinson's poetry remained relatively unknown until long after her death, and her genius has only recently been fully recognized. She had a normal desire for her work to be appreciated and published if possible, but solitude and introversion were as essential to her work as to Brontë's; and in their own times, though they were not free in the outward sense, their inner freedom was actually protected—by the very limitations we most abhor—from the kind of struggle with the world which might have destroyed their spirits. Emily Dickinson wrote to her literary mentor, Thomas Wentworth Higginson:

> I smile when you suggest that I delay "to publish"—that being foreign to my thought, as Firmament to Fin.
>
> If fame belonged to me, I could not escape her—if she did not, the longest day would pass me on the chase—and the approbation of my Dog, would forsake me—then. My Barefoot-Rank is better.

It is not, of course, the fact of publication that kills, but the attitude of our world toward it. How fortunate that her literary adviser did not understand her! In an article in the *Saturday Review of Literature* (April 19, 1975) Edward Lucie-Smith has said that poets are no longer judged by their work but by the sensational events of their lives. Suicide is becoming to the public the exciting thing about Sylvia Plath, Anne Sexton, and others.

Thus their poetry, he says, itself becomes interesting only secondarily. Any true poet would despise this sort of thing as far as his conscious attitude is concerned; but it is a grotesque extreme arising from the universal climate of our society, a climate in which the feminine qualities wither and die because nothing is judged valuable unless it is known to and approved by large numbers of people. No one remains unaffected by this climate, but most vulnerable of all are surely those very sensitive girls and women in whom there lives the spirit of potential artistic creation, and who are forced too soon into the fierce struggle for public applause. Edward Lucie-Smith ends his article with the thought that poets need the courage to say *no* to publicists and admirers. These are every bit as threatening as the old attitudes against which they protest with such vehemence. The words of Emily Dickinson, deeply heard, restore the balance as they affirm the silent integrity of the individual creative truth.

> Fame of Myself, to justify,
> All other Plaudit be
> Superfluous—An Incense
> Beyond Necessity—

Fame of Myself to lack—Although
My Name be else Supreme—
This were an Honorless
A futile Diadem—

Art is born inevitably of conflict, and the outer life of the creative genius is often tragically disordered and imposes great suffering on those close to him or her. As Jung has suggested in discussing psychology and literature, it is probably a matter of the energy which the spirit demands of one whose life is seized upon with such urgency that he must be true to his genius even if he has nothing left for other tasks and for human obligations. The one thing forbidden is the betrayal of his gift. Only the greatest of the great become complete individuals as well as supreme artists while in this world. Shakespeare was assuredly one—Dante, Blake, and Goethe, perhaps. We are concerned here, however, with the many of lesser talents, especially the women, who, however superficially *free* their lives, are enslaved by the terrible pressure of the will to *do* which kills the creative genius of the feminine and hands it over to the negative animus and his pursuit of prestige or of the shocking and spuriously original. It may be, however, that the tragic lives and psychic suffering of such devoted women are the offering which will eventually reawaken us to the values of the small, the secret, the hidden feminine muse which can produce a Brontë or a Dickinson. The conventions of society no longer protect such a one. The collective container of the family is lost and there can be no looking back, no retreat behind outer walls. We move forward to a new and challenging task—the discovery by each individual of the hidden vessel. Thus the woman poet may receive into the soil of her feminine earth the fire of the spirit and may know "the masculine and violent joy of pure creation." This is a line from the last stanza of the beautiful poem "My Sister, O My Sisters" by May Sarton, in which she writes out of her great feminine wisdom of all these things. May we remember, whether we are artists or no, that retreat from the great spirit is far more likely in our day to take the form of a busy display of pseudomasculine activity than of regression to the conventional femininity.

Every one of us, as we look back, must feel immense gratitude to those impassioned fighters whose individual *daimons* have made them spearheads of the great affirmation of freedom which has broken our collectively enforced servitude to the so-called feminine roles and is giving us equality of opportunity in every field of human endeavor. We are paying a very high price for freedom, but it cannot be evaded, and there is no remedy in a regressive renewal of the old sanctions.

Therefore, every individual woman who is capable of reflection and discrimination, and who lays claim to freedom, carries a responsibility to ask herself, "What kind of free spirit is it that breathes through me and is the dominant influence in my life?" To discover this is a task of self-knowledge which demands all the courage, honesty, and perseverance of which we are capable, and we have first to realize that real freedom from servitude comes only when one is capable of freely chosen *service*. We are freed from the *law* by which we have hitherto lived only through the choice of another binding commitment. We may do what we will only when we have learned the nature of love.

PART

II

INNER

RELATIONSHIP AND

COMMUNITY

The wisdom of the *I Ching*, the *Book of Changes*, speaks to us across the three thousand years of its life in a language that, though strange to us at first, has an extraordinarily modern accent. This is not the occasion for a detailed explanation of the structure of the book, and for our purpose it is enough to say that it contains sixty-four so-called "signs" or "hexagrams," representing different combinations of the masculine and feminine principles, the "yang" and the "yin" aspects of life, each hexagram giving wisdom for a particular situation of human life in time.

A hexagram is composed of six lines, unbroken masculine and broken feminine lines, and each of these lines refers to a special aspect of the time situation symbolized by the particular sign. Each hexagram begins with a "judgment" and an "image," the first describing the basic meaning of the whole sign, the second expressing another aspect of it in imagery. Thus the clarity of conscious judgment and the symbolism of the unconscious meet and illuminate each other throughout the book.

There are a number of hexagrams that deal specifically with different kinds of relatedness. They include: The Family, Fellowship With Men, The Marrying Maiden, Holding Together, Gathering Together, Influence, Inner Truth. It is particularly interesting to examine some of the wisdom they contain.

We begin with the natural group of The Family (Hexagram 37). The basic teaching of this sign lays down at once an unchanging essential for any kind of real relatedness between people at any level. There must be boundaries, separateness; each individual must be distinct, and there must be discrimination of function. In the Judgment it is said, "If the father is really a father and the son a son . . . if the husband is really a husband and the wife a wife, then the family is in order." How well we know in our day that the breakdown of the family comes from the loss of this wisdom! We see on all sides the woman behaving unconsciously like a man, the man a prey to feminine moods and softness, the child treated like an adult, or parents descending to childish behavior, and all the resulting misery and disorder of the indiscriminate mixture of function.

Of the six lines of the hexagram, one speaks of the child, one of woman and child, two of woman, and two of man. For the child the essential is that there should be rules of order that he may recognize from the very beginning and within which he may be entirely free. Freedom without such basic rules is a terrible burden to lay on a child. "When tempers flare up in the family, too great severity brings remorse, good fortune nonetheless. When woman and child dally and laugh, it leads in the end to humiliation." Even if we make occasional mistakes, it is better to have too much discipline than to descend to the child's level. We need to "build strong dikes" within which each individual (not only the child) can move freely, but one small hole in a dike can let in a flood.

To the woman the *I Ching* speaks in this sign with special force. "It is upon the woman of the house that the well-being of the family depends." "The atmosphere that holds the family together" depends on the woman, for she is the heart of the house, the one who nourishes it both outwardly and inwardly. "She should not follow her whims. She must attend within to the food. . . . She must attend to the nourishment of her family and to the food for the sacrifice. In this way she becomes the center of the social and religious life of the family. . . ." In Jung's language, it is the feminine principle that binds people together, the "cement" in all relationships, and this binding force of the heart may either bring people together in a true meeting or turn into the destructive and imprisoning possessiveness of the woman who follows her whims; that is to say, whose feeling consists of unconscious emotional drives instead of conscious discrimination and warmth. It is the woman, or the anima in man, who maintains the link with the depths of the unconscious, the springs of the religious instinct in man. Hence, she provides "the food for the sacrifice."

On the father of the family, the *I Ching* urges the cultivation of his own personality so that he may carry his responsibility freely and willingly and exercise authority through trustworthiness and love, never through fear. If his character is centered on inner truth, his influence in the family will operate for its well-being without conscious contriving.

"The family is society in embryo," says the *I Ching*. In every sign there are different levels of interpretation—the personal, the social and political, the cosmic; and we today may add another: the interpretation of these signs as inner situations of the individual psyche. In this particular hexagram, the advice as to discrimination of function, for instance, is profoundly valid as applied to the different aspects of a single personality. We need to be aware of the child in us, to give him or her discipline and freedom; the feminine parts of our nature, whether we be men or women, must attend to the "food" and beware of "whims"; the masculine authority must be realized through objective love and not through fear; and so on. We have not evolved any better advice in three thousand years.

We move out from containment in the family to seek Fellowship With Men (Hexagram 13). Here the necessity for discrimination, for "distinction between things," is again stressed. "Fellowship should not be a mere mingling of individuals or of things—that would be chaos, not fellowship." The lines speak of the most dangerous pitfalls. "Fellowship with men in the clan. Humiliation. There is danger here of formation of a separate faction on the basis of personal and egotistic interests." Any kind of exclusive feeling must wreck real fellowship and is something entirely different from separateness and observance of boundaries between men.

The next line warns against mistrust and suspicion. If we have mental reservations, if there is a conscious or unconscious holding back, or refusal to give of ourselves, then we will always be suspecting the same wiles in others and "the result is that one departs further and further from true fellowship." Interpreting this inwardly, we know that mistrust of ourselves is the root of all suspicion. We "condemn one group in order to unite the others"; that is, we want to accept the parts of ourselves that we like and esteem, and to reject those impulses and weaknesses which make us feel small or guilty. This rejection we project outward into condemnation of other people, feelings of superiority, or into protestations of our inferiority and worthlessness. We are thus incapable of fellowship.

The Marrying Maiden (Hexagram 54) speaks of close personal relationships based on affection:

> *Affection as the essential principle of relatedness is of the greatest importance in all relationships in the world. . . . Affection is the all-inclusive principle of union. . . . But every relationship between individuals bears within it the danger that wrong turns may be taken, leading to endless misunderstandings and disagreements. Therefore, it is necessary constantly to remain mindful of the end. If we permit ourselves to drift along, we come together and are parted again as the day may determine.*

We must "understand the transitory in the light of the eternity of the end." In other words, if our love for another person becomes an end in itself, shutting out all other loves, breeding jealousy and exclusiveness, it is not real love at all. It is by no means easy to remain "mindful of the end," of that which is beyond the personal, when we are seized by an overmastering longing for another person's love. The top line of the hexagram stresses the absolute necessity for "sacrifice" in the real sense of the word, if love is to endure. If "the woman holds the basket but there are no fruits in it," or "the man stabs the sheep, but no blood flows," then affection and love will turn in the long run to hate. The meaning of this image is that in the Chinese rite of sacrifice to the ancestors the woman presented harvest offerings, while the man slaughtered the sacrificial animal. We should say that the woman must sacrifice her possessiveness, must offer her "fruits," let go of her children, her *demand* to be loved, while a man must sacrifice his aggressive instincts, his sensuality in its blind, unfeeling form.

We come now to the hexagram that deals specifically with the coming together of men in communities or groups. The *I Ching* points out that there is in man a need for relationship in groups as well as between individuals. In our day, owing to the breakdown of the traditional family, social, and religious values, and still more because of the split between intellect and instinct, between conscious and unconscious, in the collective psyche, this need has become almost frenzied. "Togetherness," that frightening word, has replaced relationship and has become a cultural idea. Study groups, conferences, camps, "workshops," human "laboratories," spring up on every side to meet a very real human need, but they have also their danger. Often designed to help people toward self-knowledge, they become for many a protection against that very thing, a running away from the essentially lonely tasks of facing the dark sides of the individual soul. Therefore, very great care and awareness are needed before one joins any kind of group. "Will this mean running away for me," one must ask, "or will it bring real support and new consciousness?" The essential inner journey must be made alone, but all of us need support and relatedness with others of like mind; and it is fatally easy to mistake dependence, a blind acceptance of the opinions of others, for real mutual support, for the humility that respects another's view but never swallows it whole. We all long to fly from loneliness to "togetherness," but the only real cure for loneliness is to accept the "aloneness" of the spirit, and then, to our astonishment, real relatedness, real friendship, will come to our doorstep, wherever we may be.

The I Ching says of itself that it speaks only to the "superior" man, which in Jung's language means the "conscious" man, and the wisdom of Holding Together (Hexagram 8) and Gathering Together (Hexagram 45) would mean little to those who seek community for escapist reasons. It speaks to those who seek a holding together with others of like mind as free individuals, to those who are striving for the wholeness that Jung has called "individuation."

Both hexagrams begin by emphasizing the necessity for a leader, a person around whom others unite. The ancient Chinese culture was feudal, but the validity of the principle remains. The elected representative in a democracy must take up and carry the responsibility of leadership for his term of office, but he is protected as far as is collectively possible from identifying personally with his power. In every kind of group, even that which is a gathering of free and conscious individuals, there must be leadership—the kind about which Charles Williams wrote so beautifully when he described the "excellent absurdity" of one man acting as a center for others. He must at all times be aware of his ultimate unimportance and dispensability, must be wholly aware that he is not the center, but merely a focal point through which, if this task has been laid upon him, others may recognize *the* center within themselves. In expressing this, Charles Williams shows himself entirely at one with the ancient teaching of the *I Ching*.

In the commentary on one of the lines in the sign Holding Together, it is said of the leader:

> *Those who come to him he accepts, those who do not come are allowed to go their own way. He invites none, flatters none—all come of their own free will. In this way there develops a voluntary dependence among those who hold to him. They do not have to be constantly on their guard but may express their opinions openly. Police measures are not necessary. . . . The same principle of freedom is valid for life in general. We should not woo favor from people. If a man cultivates within himself the purity and strength that are necessary for one who is the center of a fellowship, those who are meant for him come of their own accord.*

If there is this kind of freedom in a community, then each member of it will begin to find real leadership within himself, the impersonal purity and strength, the center, the "Self" displacing the ego's leadership. Around this center first of all his own personality will "gather," and it will then be felt by all those who are "meant for him." "This leader must first of all be collected within himself."

In another hexagram called Following (Hexagram 17), it is said that all those who are followed must themselves know how to follow. When the situation requires any one of us to lead, we must have the courage and humility to do so, and when it is time to be led, this also we accept in freedom and true independence. The one requires the other; indeed, they beget each other.

The first line in the sign Holding Together (Hexagram 8) speaks of the fundamental sincerity that is the essential for all relationship: "This attitude, symbolized by a full earthen bowl, in which the content is everything and the empty form nothing, shows itself not in clever words but through the strength of what lies within the speaker." The second line points out that, if we are seeking any kind of personal advantage from our association with a group, then we "lose" ourselves. In other words, we are merely bolstering up unconscious demands; we are not individuals anymore.

The third line reads, "You hold together with the wrong people." This is a warning against false intimacy with people who do not meet us on our own deepest level. This does not mean that we may not enjoy the company of such people, but the commentary insists with surprising force on the danger of *intimacy* in the wrong place. "We must beware of being drawn into false intimacy through force of habit. . . . Maintaining sociability without intimacy is the only right attitude . . . because otherwise we should not be free to enter into relationship with people of our own kind." In our terms, to reveal ourselves, our thoughts and feelings to someone who does not understand our basic values is not only pointless —it exposes us to invasion by superficial attitudes and literally corrupts or steals away our energy, dissipating it, or imprisoning it, so that we have nothing left to give to the true relationship.

Another line warns against too long a delay in giving "complete and full devotion" to the group that we have recognized to be the carrier of our real values. The hexagram is concerned with groups, but we may interpret this line as also warning of those moments when we are capable of a new and more complete commitment to the way of individuation, moments when we have to make a vital choice. "If we have missed the right moment for union and go on hesitating to give complete and full devotion, we shall regret the error when it is too late." A dream will often bring to consciousness this necessity for a choice and, if we refuse it, it may be a long time before the opportunity returns.

The hexagram of Gathering Together (Hexagram 45) is very similar to that of Holding Together, but it deals with one other aspect of the subject—the danger of strife and conflict within a group and of "robbery" from without. The I Ching says that there is one strong defense against these splitting attacks from within and from without—a constant watchfulness and foresight. We must *expect* these things. "Human woes usually come as a result of unexpected events against which we are not forearmed." We are continually thrown by our own moods and weaknesses into destructive attitudes, because, when things are going well, we cease to expect any setback, and when it comes, we fall into discouragement and seek for scapegoats. In the first line we are told what to do in such a case. "If you are sincere but not to the end, there will sometimes be confusion, sometimes gathering together. If you call out, then after one grasp of the hand you can laugh again. Regret not."

A beautiful passage from the commentary on another line may end our study of these two signs.

> In the time of gathering together, we should make no arbitrary choice of the way. There are secret forces at work, leading together those who belong together. We must yield to this attraction; then we make no mistakes. Where inner relationships exist, no great preparations and formalities are necessary. People understand one another forthwith, just as the Divinity graciously accepts a small offering if it comes from the heart.

There is a passage in Man and His Symbols in the section by Marie-Louise von Franz that sums up this wisdom in modern terms:

> It is ultimately the Self that orders and regulates one's human relationships, so long as the conscious ego takes the trouble to detect the delusive projections and deals with these inside himself instead of outside. It is in this way that spiritually attuned and similarly oriented people find their way to one another, to create a group that cuts across all the usual social and organizational affiliations. Such a group is not in conflict with others; it is merely different and independent. The consciously realized process of individuation thus changes a person's relationships. The fa-

miliar bonds such as kinship or common interests are replaced by a different type of unity—a bond through the Self.

In the sign Dispersion or Dissolution (Hexagram 59), the necessity for dissolving these old familiar bonds to collective groups is stressed, so that the new and free type of union may be born. "He dissolves his bond with his group. Supreme good fortune. Dispersion leads in turn to accumulation. This is something that ordinary men do not think of." In another sign (Decrease, Hexagram 41) there is a line, "When three people journey together, their number decreases by one. When one man journeys alone, he finds a companion." Only when a man can stand alone does he find the real unity with others.

Influence (Hexagram 31) is concerned with the ways in which one may safely influence others or be influenced by them. The image for this sign is a mountain with a sunken peak holding the water of a lake. The mountain in the I Ching is the symbol of keeping still; the lake stands for joy. If we know how to keep still inwardly, others may be nourished by our joy and we will be receptive to any true influence from without. The lines point out some of the pitfalls: if a man should run "precipitately after all the persons whom he would like to influence" or "yield immediately to every whim of those in whose service he stands," then the result is inevitably humiliation. The most superficial of all ways of trying to influence others is through talk with nothing real behind it, mere tongue wagging. However:

When the quiet power of a man's own character is at work, the effects produced are right. All those who are receptive to the vibrations of such a spirit will then be influenced. Influence over others should not express itself as a conscious and willed effort to manipulate them. Through practicing such conscious incitement, one becomes wrought up and is exhausted by the eternal stress and strain. Moreover, the effects produced are then limited to those on whom one's thoughts are consciously fixed.

Finally in the hexagram of Inner Truth (Hexagram 61) there is a line that most beautifully expresses this deepest level of all in the relationship of one man with another. The text is "A crane calling in the shade. Its young answers it. I have a good goblet. I will share it with you."

And the commentary:

This refers to the involuntary influence of a man's inner being upon persons of kindred spirit. . . . The crane may be quite hidden when it sounds its call. . . . Where there is a joyous mood, there a comrade will appear to share a glass of wine. . . . Whenever a feeling is voiced with truth and frankness, whenever a deed is the clear expression of sentiment, a mysterious and far-reaching influence is exerted. At first it acts on those who are inwardly receptive. But the circle grows larger and larger. The root of all influence lies in one's inner being. . . . Any deliberate intention of an effect would only destroy the possibility of producing it.

Confucius said about this line:

The superior man abides in his room. If his words are well spoken, he meets with assent at a distance of more than a thousand miles. How much more then from near by! If the superior man abides in his room and his words are not well spoken, he meets with contradiction at a distance of more than a thousand miles. How much more then from near by! . . . Through words and deeds the superior man moves heaven and earth. Must one not, then, be cautious?

MONEY AND THE FEMININE PRINCIPLE OF RELATEDNESS

The word "money" is derived from the Latin *moneta*, meaning mint or money, and was originally the name of the goddess in whose temple in Rome money was coined. It is significant indeed that the goddess from whose temple, from whose womb, so to speak, sprang the coinage of our civilization has sunk into obscurity and is forgotten, while the money which was dedicated to her has acquired an ever increasing autonomous power and is worshiped unashamedly as an end in itself.

It was certainly not by chance that the ancient Romans set their mint in the temple of a goddess and not of a god—for money is a symbolic means of exchange and therefore belongs to the feminine principle of relatedness. If, therefore, the "goddess" is missing, that third transpersonal factor which gives meaning to every exchange between human beings, whether physical, emotional, spiritual, or financial, then we are in acute danger, for the thing or the experience has lost its connection with the symbol, the meaning sinks into the unconscious, and we are inevitably possessed by some kind of autonomous, power-filled complex. Thus the love of the divinity at the heart of exchange turns into the love of money itself which, in the words of Timothy in one of his epistles, is "the root of all evil." Money itself is not, of course, evil. It is an essential for any kind of civilized society; but the minute our attitude to money is divorced from its meaning as an exchange between people involving *feeling* values, then we begin to love money for its own sake or for the sake of that which we can gain from it, either possessions or security or, worst of all, power. It hardly needs to be added that to maintain our sense of the symbol in our money dealing requires of us a very high degree of consciousness indeed.

Charles Williams, in one of the poems in his Arthurian cycle, wrote of the beauty inherent in the simple exchange of goods and services and described the coming of the coins which were to symbolize it. The poem is called "Bors to Elayne: The King's Coins." Sir Bors is married to Elayne in this poem, and he sings of the beauty of her hands as she bakes bread to feed the men who have been working in the fields. He particularly stresses the thumbs, the unique feature of the human hand ("the thumbs are muscled with the power of good will"), and we feel them as the symbol of that conscious exchange by which human beings truly live. In this exchange, Bors says, *"none only earn and none only pay."* Elayne, the lady, kneads bread with her thumbs. The beautiful meaning of the word "lady" is, in fact, "kneader of bread." The men sow and harvest the wheat; thus they both earn and pay for the bread by their labors, as Elayne and her women, by their work of baking and distributing the bread, both earn and pay for the wheat and the labor of the men. It is, as C. S. Lewis says, "the honourable and blessed" exchange of one kind of service, one kind of work, for another.

Bors, however, has come from London where, with the growth of civilization, a new means of exchange has come into being. "The king has set up his mint by Thames. He has struck coins." Bors knows that this is a necessary thing, but he has been having bad dreams. The coins have the king's head on one side and a dragon on the other. It is as though already they have acquired a life of their own, these little dragons, and the king's head (the royal consciousness of the Self, in symbolic language) is dead. The "dragonlets . . . scuttle and scurry between towns and towns," / their eyes "leer and peer, and the house roofs under their weight / creak and break" in Bors's dream. Kay, the king's steward, the businessman of Arthur's court, says, "Streams are bridged and mountains of ridged space / tunnelled; gold dances deftly across frontiers. / The

poor have choice of purchase, the rich of rents. . . . Money is the medium of exchange." Taliessin, the king's poet, however, is afraid. His
hand shakes when he touches the dragons. "I am afraid of the little
loosed dragons. / When the means are autonomous, they are deadly;
when words / escape from verse they hurry to rape souls; when sensation
slips from intellect, expect the tyrant."

The archbishop in the poem replies that even when God is hidden
the truth of exchange remains. I take him to mean that an individual
may still hold to the symbol no matter what collective values prevail. He
goes on, "We must lose our own ends . . . my friend's shelter for me,
mine for him . . . the wealth of the self is the health of the self exchanged. . . . Money is a medium of exchange." The difference between the archbishop's statement and Kay's is profound. "Money," says
the archbishop, "is a means of exchange" (for each person)—not "the
medium of exchange."

Bors ends with a question to his lady and a prayer. Compact, he says,
is becoming contract; and he adds that man now only earns or only pays.
Then he asks, "What without coinage or with coinage can be saved?" He
ends, "Pray, mother of children, pray for the coins." It is not the coinage
itself which is the issue; the evil is the loss in man of the link to the
feeling values of exchange. Therefore it is the "mother" who must pray—
the woman whose very being depends on relatedness.

A compact is, literally, an agreement based on feeling values; it means
a coming together in peace, cum pace. A contract is a legal or financial
agreement which binds outwardly, regardless of the human feelings involved. So, when compact becomes contract within us, men begin to
earn without paying or pay without earning, and money is divorced from
the meaning of exchange.

If we hold one gold or silver coin in our hands and really see it, what a
beautiful thing it is. If we still used gold coins stamped with the king's
head on one side and the dragon on the other, it would surely be easier to
feel with joy the symbolism of the Self in every earning and every paying.
(I have one gold coin still—a 1910 half sovereign with the king's head
and St. George with the dragon.) Even our debased coinage retains ves-
tiges of the importance of the symbols, reduced to mere signs though they

may be—the great man's head and the eagle of the twenty-five-cent piece, for instance—and all coins have the roundness of the whole. Our paper money is a mere convenient token of true money; it still has the head, but the pictures of public buildings which replace the old animal symbols betray the poverty of our attitudes. The dragons have indeed escaped, and in the unconscious they make an unholy alliance with the sterile severed head; thus men watch helplessly the "leering and peering" of the loosed power. "When the means are autonomous they are deadly." When words escape from poetry, when the mint emerges from the temple, then souls are raped; speech becomes jargon, paying becomes bribing, earning becomes joyless necessity, and the acts of exchange which are the glory of humanity become mere bargains. (*It would be hard to say whether words or coins are ahead nowadays in the race to destroy souls.*)

That good old English word "stock" has many beautiful meanings, all derived from the original one of the main trunk of a tree or plant onto which grafts are made. It means too the store of raw material, of goods which are the basis of new development. "He comes of good stock," we say, speaking of a man's roots—of the raw material of his inherited personality. When autonomous money becomes the stock upon which the life of a man or a society is grafted, the rot begins. We forget the ancient and beautiful image of the marketplace, where fruits of the earth and products of the human hand were exchanged, when we talk of the money markets and stock exchanges of the world. In these money is made to breed and breed only itself. People buy and sell rye or wheat, for instance, without the remotest connection with the crops growing in the fields, even in thought. Something is to be had for nothing by the clever playing of the markets, and this is the absolute negation of exchange. The Usurers in Dante's Inferno were deep in Nether Hell on the sterile burning sand. One commentator has written that they were there because they made money breed—money, which is in itself sterile.

Under this weight of paper and the inflation it brings, our rooftops are indeed creaking and breaking. This "brood of carriers," as Taliessin calls the little loosed dragons, bring power to their owners, power and more power, until the good stock from which they sprang is wholly forgotten and people would think us crazy if we reminded them in this context that the word "share" had a blessed human meaning.

Money was a most wonderful invention of the human mind. It brought to man an enormous extension of freedom from the immediate necessities of mere existence. "The poor have choice of purchase, the rich of rents." At every step along the way of civilization energy was set free by money, and people could choose how they would spend this energy. They could and did choose creation, discovery, and growth of all kinds. But in more and more people the desire to possess the gold lured that energy to itself and the severed head, and the greed of the dragon overran the values of the heart and spirit.

Modern humankind is increasingly aware of this terrible predicament. There have been countless genuine and courageous efforts to counteract this autonomous breeding. The revolutionaries have attempted to solve the problem by a complete overthrow of personal ownership—only to create the worse horror of the manipulation of the money forces by a heartless all-powerful state for the so-called good of the many, and the concentration of this tremendous power in the hands of a very few.

Democracies, with varying success, and in spite of their muddles and corruptions, have tried to find a means of controlling the greed of the few, caring for the old and sick and unfortunate, searching, at least, for a social equity which will not destroy individual freedom of exchange. But they have proved powerless to stop the breeding, the inflations and depressions.

Groups of individuals have sought to free themselves by pooling all their money and living in communities. But most of the members are not inwardly free from the greed which they seek to combat and are not yet capable of free exchange, so their well-meant efforts are an escape, not an affirmation. One cannot go back to the simple life until one has taken up the responsibility for money and learned the nature of exchange through both earning and paying. I do not believe that any commune can survive for long in our times when money is pooled. Religious communities through the centuries thrived because of the dedication which meant an inward earning and paying through an intense devotion to the symbolic life, but in our day individuals must increasingly take up their lonely responsibilities, and the temptation to escape from these through so-called community is very strong.

The lonely hermits were forerunners in the desert of what eventually a conscious person had to achieve *inwardly*. But no person today may legitimately renounce money outwardly until he or she has a true understanding of what inner poverty is. If money is *taken* from someone, then he is tested indeed; for the very poor it is as difficult as for the very rich to hold to the values of true exchange.

It is a very great thing that so many young people today are seeing clearly the horrible evils of a money-dominated society. Their danger is that, in so rightly rejecting its values, they may also reject the responsibility for that which money symbolizes—the earning and paying for which it stands. They speak of and indeed show love and concern for each other, but too often the "love" is confined to those of like mind and like age—and is therefore merely an extended self-concern. Exchange is never exclusive. Moreover, the insidious belief may creep in that "society" owes them a living—that money *itself* is evil. Therefore they feel anything can be demanded or even stolen from others, especially from impersonal organizations, without obligation either to earn or to pay. This, of course, is as complete a denial of human exchange as any of the financiers are guilty of.

What, then, is the answer for the ordinary citizen, aware of the evils, but seemingly powerless to alter anything? As with every other collective problem, there can be no outer solution without the transformation of individuals. There is, therefore, the imperative need for each person to enter upon the hard way of scrutinizing with ever increasing consciousness his or her own personal attitudes to money.

So let us look closely at some of the signs whereby we may recognize in our ordinary transactions either the symbol at work or the insidious power, greed or fear born of the autonomy of money within us.

We may begin by considering the very common pitfalls into which married couples fall, not because married people are any more unconscious than anyone else, but simply because marriage between a man and a woman is the greatest of all human symbols of exchange between the two basic forces of the universe—the creative and the receptive, the male and the female, the head and the dragon. Therefore the money dealings between the partners in a marriage are apt to show up very clearly their conscious and unconscious attitudes toward the meaning of exchange. I am inclined to say that married people who are seeking consciousness are extremely lucky in having this clearly defined problem to work on! Of course people living alone have exactly the same attitudes to contend with, but it is very much easier for them to bury the whole thing and imagine that they are not at all unconscious about money matters. Even friends living together and sharing expenses are not forced to confront at every turn the age-old assumptions in the unconscious about husbands' "rights" or the modern emergence of women's "rights." A single person usually has his or her own money and responsibilities, but it would be good for every unmarried person to think deeply about how he or she would feel about money in the event of marriage. It is not by chance that Williams's poem begins with that beautiful imagery of the essence of exchange between Bors and his wife Elayne—between his men and her women—the collective exchange, be it noted, springing from the individual one.

There are several symptoms of the betrayal of exchange in marriage. First there is the old and still very powerful male assumption, in spite of all protestations to the contrary, that he, being the chief money provider, owns all the money and will give to his wife sufficient for her needs. Usually he will say or imply, "I can't understand what she is fussing about. She can have anything she wants within my means. She knows that." He does not see the power motive at the back of this. He will be the bountiful giver. He is most willing to pay for his wife's pleasure, but he does not really admit that she earns and pays by her work and her childbearing and her love and that she needs to feel that she has money which is *wholly* her own, so that she may choose her ways of spending without reference to him should she so wish. Let it be added that often the woman's unconscious is equally to blame with its tendency to welcome absorption into another's life. A woman so often takes the easy way of complaining instead of standing up for her values (not rights), so deep is the inherited sense of inferiority with its temptation to avoid all responsibility. Quite often, too, the opposite may happen. The man refuses all responsibility and hands over the management of their joint money to the woman. She doles it out to him. The animus may be delighted, but woe to the chances of exchange in that marriage.

More common in our time, and particularly in the first warm and genuine sharing of a new marriage, is the declaration by both man and woman, "We shall pool all we have in a joint account and have no disagreements about how it shall be spent." It may well be so, but these people with all their manifest good will reckon without the immensely powerful symbolic meaning of money itself. It means *exchange*—it does not mean mixing. If the two people concerned have really arrived at a very high degree of the inner separation which is individuation, all well and good; but I need hardly say that such a situation is extremely rare. For almost all there is a hidden danger which over the years can undermine a potentially fine and growing partnership. One question usually opens a person's eyes. Have you thought that in making this arrangement you effectually destroy any possibility of ever truly giving your wife or husband a present? The question may sound superficial—in fact it lays bare the whole deadly business of how we are misled by so many seemingly generous impulses to the evasion of the responsibilities of individual exchange. Sooner or later it is a hundred to one that the partners will begin to feel, unconsciously if not consciously, either a resentment because he wants something and is not free to buy it, or a guilt that she has spent money which was not wholly hers.

A joint account for joint expenses which can be budgeted is obviously excellent; for the rest, unless each partner has complete individual control of his or her share, without obligation even to tell the partner what he or she does with it, the dignity of exchange is easily lost.

When the woman has or earns money of her own and retains control of it, things are easier, given the essential good will. But if one or the other partner has much more money than is needed for a moderate standard of living, then other dangers arise. A woman's animus, operating out of seemingly clear-cut principles, as he is apt to do, and unconscious of his power drives, may insist on fifty-fifty proceedings when it is quite unsuitable. A man's anima may fog everything up and obscure his power motives so that all the true issues are lost. Each person in this challenging quest for the true nature of exchange must take into account the state of consciousness of the other and discover where to stand up and where to let go. There are no rules; the only vital thing is the fundamental honesty of the will to exchange, to earn and to pay—the refusal to dominate, to depend, or to mix. If we do not do this in money matters, we most surely don't do it elsewhere.

In the area of wages and salaries, the issue is clear. When there is true exchange between employer and employed it is a beautiful thing—the master respecting the skills and service of the man, the man respecting the master's knowledge and willingness to take responsibility and risk. It can still today be a relationship full of that dignity and true equality so easily lost the minute all start fighting for their "rights" instead of *for the fairness of exchange*. As soon as earning and paying become bargaining, the issues turn ugly; the love of money in both employers and employees takes over as an end in itself. Thus the meaningless spiral of inflation continues. The word "inflation" in this context means the blowing up of the artificial value of money disconnected from the goods it represents. The financiers see this entirely in an outer sense; it is in fact a symptom of the ever increasing gap between money and its root in the ground of human relatedness.

The only thing we can certainly do about it is to give a great deal of attention to our individual attitudes when we employ anybody (even if it be a single cleaning woman), and when we are employed. Is our payment to an employee also an earning of his service on the feeling level? When we accept our earnings, have we really paid in full for them, and do we recognize the work of our employers which has earned the payment he makes to us? It grows more and more difficult, of course, to hold to these things in proportion to the size of the business or the institution, when employers are entirely unknown as people and have no notion of who their employees are. Nevertheless, what an enormous difference the attitude of the man at the top has on even a big organization. It creates an atmosphere by which even the most obscure employee will be influenced.

One can usually tell by the atmosphere of a store whether the owner cares for the values of exchange in his money dealing or whether he cares only for money itself.

Of course, no matter what the general state of affairs is, one may come across individuals anywhere in whom this beauty shines. I suppose every woman among us can remember instances on her shopping trips when she has been served by a saleswoman who is truly concerned, not just to sell her any old thing, but to find the coat or the dress that is exactly right, and this is accomplished for obviously personal as well as business reasons. We come away not only delighted with our acquisition but with a feeling of real exchange between people, and the money which passes is for the moment truly connected to that for which it stands. *In our hearts Elayne has baked bread for the reapers of the grain.*

The enormous size, however, of so many corporations and institutions is as nothing to the size of the state, that abstract entity to which we pay our taxes and on which we for the most part can safely vent the resentments and guilts born of our own unfaced shadow qualities—our own evasions of the responsibilities of true exchange. People who would cry out in horror when a man cheats his neighbor or refuses to pay his debts may grin when telling you how they have just hatched up a new plot to evade taxation. I am not, of course, talking about the many entirely legitimate ways of reducing one's tax load. That would be foolish sentimentality and scrupulosity. There is a thin line between that and dishonesty, but for anyone who thinks of money as a symbol of exchange, it can be a very clear one. If we really think deeply, taxation emerges as one of the greatest ideas that humankind has ever conceived. It is the means whereby people live in community with each other while still retaining freedom of choice in most of their spending and earning. Without taxation there must be dictatorship or anarchy. As on all levels of exchange, the sacrifice of a degree of freedom ensures the essential freedom.

The tax evaders, who often produce lofty motives for their actions, reply that, since they disapprove so strongly of the ways in which the government spends public money, they will evade as much as they can. Could any reasoning be more specious? Do we refuse to pay a debt because we disapprove of the way our creditor spends his money? Our taxes are the debt which every man who lives in a civilized society owes to every one of the millions of his fellow citizens. It may be replied that we do not incur this debt willingly. Most surely we do, whenever we post a letter, use a road, accept a penny of welfare or unemployment money, or call the fire department or the police.

As to the often unjust, mistaken, and corrupt ways in which tax money is spent, it is we, each one of us, who carry the final responsibility for the government in power, whichever way we have voted; for it has been truly said that a country has the government it deserves; that is, the government is a reflection of the dominant attitudes in the lives of its individual citizens. Whoever we vote for, if in our personal lives we do not adhere to the honesty and feeling values of true exchange in all our earning and paying, including our tax paying, then we are contributing most effectively to the greed and hatred and power seeking which produce such things as militarism and the corruption of "lobbies." It is futile to fight such things if one is all the time practicing them under cover of righteous indignation, and the very last way to stop them is to withhold that which is a great affirmation of every human being's responsibility for all his fellows.

If a person believes that the government has betrayed the trust of the people, he has, in a democracy, many means of fighting. If he or she is convinced that only rebellion will serve, then let him or her refuse all money payments and go to prison or leave the country.

Our dealings with impersonal entities such as the state, corporations, institutions and businesses can provide us with a searchlight into many of the unnoticed shadows within us—think, for instance, of the insidious temptations of the expense account, a most safe and easy way to defraud —safer even than semiconscious money exchanges with one's parents or wife or husband or children. The state and the corporation are not pure abstractions; behind them all are individual people, no matter how hard it may be to imagine this. If we lose track of the clear beauty of exchange in our attitudes to these collectivities, we may be very sure there is something wrong in all our relationships—in all the closest and most valued exchanges of our lives.

Perhaps the most universal fear in us all is *the fear of the loss of security.*

The smallest knowledge of the psyche awakens us to the fact that only by facing this fear and by giving *a fundamental consent to insecurity*, in any context, can we hope to know real freedom from anxiety. This is as true in relationships to money as it is to everything else. Anxiety about money is in no way dependent on the amount of money a person possesses. It is often much stronger in those who have plenty of money than in those who have little. It is in truth especially hard for the rich (and not only the rich in money) to enter the peace of the "Kingdom of Heaven," whose very definition is "exchange" on earth, because to do so we must accept, embrace even, insecurity on every other level of being, a thing which the rich (even the rich in spirit) often fear more than anything.

"The wealth of the self is the health of the self exchanged," says the archbishop in Williams's poem. The word "health" is derived from the same root as wholeness. Only awareness of this can save us from the pursuit of security, possessions and, finally, power through money as an end in itself. "When the means are autonomous they are deadly."

When we dream about money, it is often clearly a symbol of psychic energy. We may learn a lot from our dreams of money as to how we are spending our inner energy—whether we hoard it, make bargains with it, steal energy from others, or earn and pay in the freedom of exchange.

Finally we may think about the free giving and free taking of money. To give it or take it without any unconscious strings attached is no easy thing, and on one level it appears that we have to free ourselves absolutely from any thought of earning or of paying when we make a gift or receive one. The giver must have no ulterior earning motive; the gift must not buy good will; the recipient must never feel it is payment for value personally given.

There is, however, another level upon which any free giver or taker is most precisely and accurately earning and paying. It is the level from which Christ spoke when he said, "Owe no man anything but to love one another." In all our money dealing we symbolically incur and pay this universal debt if only we will dare to be aware of it. When we are thus aware, we shall give instinctively neither too little nor too much.

Indeed, perhaps we could sum up this whole matter by saying that when in every money exchange we *both* earn and pay, pay and earn, then our earning and paying become the free giving and free taking whereby money enters the "temple" once more, and the dragons are at peace with the head of the king in the pure gold of the human heart.

SUFFERING

"Suffering" is a word used to express so many kinds of experience that its precision of meaning has been lost. The Latin verb *ferre* means "to bear," "to carry," and "suffer" derives from it, with the prefix "sub" meaning "under." This is reminiscent of the term "undercarriage"—that which bears the weight of a vehicle above the wheels—which is an apt image of the meaning of suffering in human life.

In contrast to the word "suffer," such terms as "affliction," "grief," and "depression" all bring images of weight bearing *down*. To be afflicted is to be struck down by a blow (*fligere*: to strike). "Grief" is derived from *gravare*, and to be depressed is to be pressed down. Only when we suffer in the full sense of the word do we *carry* the weight. A man may say, "I am so terribly depressed, I can't bear the suffering," when in fact he may not be suffering at all, but simply lying down under the weight of outer circumstances or inner mood.

There are, then, two kinds of experiences which we call suffering— that which is totally unproductive, the neurotic state of meaningless depression, and that which is the essential condition of every step on the way to what C. G. Jung has called individuation. Perhaps these images of weight under which we fall and lie in self-pity, or of weight which we carry in full consciousness, may be a guideline in moments of darkness.

The blows of great affliction or grief are comparatively rare, but day-to-day onslaughts of hurt feelings, black moods, exhaustion, resentment and, most deadly of all, false guilt, are the training ground, and nothing is too small to offer us an opportunity to choose between suffering and depression.

Deeply ingrained in the infantile psyche is the conscious or unconscious assumption that the cure for depression is to replace it with pleasant, happy feelings, whereas the only valid cure for any kind of depression lies in the acceptance of real suffering. To climb out of it any other way is simply a palliative, laying the foundations for the next depression. Nothing whatever has happened to the soul. The roots of all our neuroses lie here, in the conflict between the longing for growth and freedom and our incapacity or refusal to pay the price in suffering of the kind which challenges the supremacy of the ego's demands. This is the crux of the matter (and we may pause here to recognize the exact meaning of the word "crux"). The ego will endure the worst agonies of neurotic misery rather than one moment of consent to the death of even a small part of its demand or its sense of importance.

We can do something toward tracking down some of the continual evasions of the ego by uncovering our fear of humiliation. From this fear of degradation in our own eyes or in the eyes of others, real or imagined, comes a dead weight of moods and depression. For the truly humble person no humiliation exists. It is impossible to humiliate him or for him to feel humiliation, for "grades" and prestige, questions of his own merit or demerit, have no more meaning for him. But the way to humility lies through the pain of accepted humiliation. In the moment of picking it up and carrying it without any movement toward self-justification, we cease to be humiliated and begin to suffer. In this context, it is well to realize the extent to which we are all open in the unconscious to the present collective worship of what we may call "grades."

Worship is not too strong a word. The more the conscious ideal of the equality of man is proclaimed on the wrong levels, the more desperate becomes the unconscious urge to assert the difference, and the yearning for prestige of all kinds breaks loose from the natural hierarchies of being into the struggles of the ego for ascendancy. The inequalities of class in the aristocratic age, absurd though we may call them, were certainly less conducive to neurosis than the gradings of money, academic prowess, I.Q.s, and A's, B's, and C's in every department of life, which can so dominate our personal unconscious that we are busy grading our weaknesses day in and day out—a very different thing from searching them out and carrying them. The poison of false values thus invades every corner of the psyche. A question to be constantly asked in moods of weakness and depression is, "Am I grading myself or am I recognizing the golden opportunity to suffer and so to deny to some small degree the ego's demands for prestige?"

The worst stumbling block of all derives from this grading. There was no guilt involved in being born into this or that social class, but nowadays we are beset on every side by a false guilt which is inverted pride. If we do not rate a B or at least a C in every department of life, then we deem ourselves guilty. The puritanical strain in our heritage reinforces this until we can even allow our work on our inner life to engender a false sense of guilt about our physical as well as our emotional weaknesses.

Of course on one level it is true that any kind of symptom, physical or psychological, is a clue to the working of the unconscious which should be followed up at the right time. But if we feel this deadly kind of guilt it simply means that we cannot accept our human condition, that we have given way to hubris and are saying unconsciously, "I ought to be like God, free of all weakness," forgetting what happened to God himself on the cross. The clues are to be worked upon, but the symptom itself is something to be wholly and freely accepted without egotistic guilt or any *demand* to be freed from it.

Hope for release is another thing, both natural and right, as also are the exterior efforts to come out of the sickness or mood. We are not excused from ordinary common sense by the fact that we accept the suffering and demand no release. In fact the two attitudes are one, and real acceptance will lead us to seek the appropriate help, whether medical skill in illness, the support of friends in grief, rest in exhaustion, work either physical or psychological in depression. Thus we begin to build the "undercarriage" of suffering upon which the superstructure of our lives may securely rest and under which the wheels may move freely over the earth. The four-wheeled chariot is an ancient symbol of the Incarnation, and the thought of suffering as the undercarriage fits perfectly into this image. Suffering is that which carries the weight of the vehicle, distributing it over the fourfold wheels so that the driver may stand in safety and move toward his chosen goal.

However great our efforts may be to achieve this conscious attitude to suffering, we cannot succeed without an awareness that, in spite of apparent senselessness, there is always an implicit universal meaning even in the carrying of small miseries. Every time a person exchanges neurotic depression for real suffering, he or she is sharing to some small degree in the carrying of the suffering of mankind, in bearing a tiny part of the darkness of the world. Such a one is released from his small personal concern into a sense of *meaning*. One may not be consciously thinking in those terms, but the transition can immediately be recognized by the disappearance of the frustrated pointlessness of mood and depression. It is as though we become aware of a new dimension. Meaning has entered the experience.

We may be emotionally moved and filled with horror and pity when we hear of the tragedies of human lives at a distance, but the emotions lift no burden, they carry nothing. In contrast, the smallest consent to the fierce, sharp pain of objective suffering in the most trivial-seeming matter may have an influence, as the Chinese sage puts it, "at a distance of a thousand miles." We may be entirely certain that some burden somewhere is lightened by our effort. Close at hand the effects are immediately visible. Those around us may know nothing of what is happening, but a weight is lifted from the atmosphere, or someone we love is set free to be himself, and the sufferer acquires a new clarity of vision and sensitivity to another's need. Nothing is as blinding as neurotic self-pity. We walk around in a fog.

There is a familiar example of the difference between objective suffering and subjective emotional reaction in its effect on others, which many people have experienced at some time in their lives if they have been seriously ill. A nurse, or anyone else who is close to another's pain, physical or psychic, if she reacts with intense personal emotion to the patient's misery, will either repress what she cannot bear and become hard and unfeeling, or else will increase the sick one's burden through her unconscious identification. A true nurse, by contrast, is always deeply concerned; she is compassionate (which means objectively "suffering with") but not invaded by emotional reactions. She is herself changed by the experience through the love that lives beyond emotion. The patient can literally be saved by this kind of "carrying" by another, but can be swamped and pushed deeper into misery by the unconscious reactions of those around him or her, however well they may be disguised. The difference is subtle but absolutely distinct when experienced.

Just as there is no cure for an inferior kind of love except a greater and more conscious love, so there is no cure for inferior so-called suffering except a greater kind of suffering. It is possible by intense conscious attention to pass through this door into the fiercer suffering which is linked to the whole, and then a strange thing may happen. We have lifted the weight and, instead of being crushed by it, we find it is extraordinarily light—"My yoke is easy, my burden is light." The pain remains but it is more like the piercing of a sword than a weight. "Yea, a sword shall pierce through thy own soul also, that the thoughts of many hearts may be revealed" (Luke 2:35). These are the prophetic words of the wise old man Simeon, spoken to Mary when she took her newborn child to the temple. We have shed blood, the sacrificial blood, and so we can experience joy, not just pleasant feelings and escape.

There is in man a fear of joy as keen as the fear of suffering pain, because true joy precludes the pleasant feeling of self-importance just as suffering precludes all the comforts of self-pity. No man can know the one without the other. It is important here to discriminate between the spurious joy of the martyr complex and the joy which is on the other side of the cross. Christ was not a martyr, going singing to his death. If we catch ourselves feeling noble on account of our sufferings, we may be perfectly sure that we are simply at the old trick of climbing out of depression into pleasant feeling—all the more dangerous because it is camouflaged as noble.

Real suffering belongs to innocence, not guilt. As long as we feel misery because we are full of remorse and guilt or shame over our weakness, all we experience is a loss of vital energy and no transformation takes place. But the minute we accept objectively the guilt and shame, the *innocent* part of us begins to suffer, the weight becomes a sword. We bleed, and the energy flows back into us on a deeper and more conscious level. This is real repentance as opposed to ego-centered shame, for it involves the recognition of the true guilt which lies always in our evasions of objective awareness.

For Christians, it is easy to give lip service to the "innocent victim," to Christ carrying in innocence the sin and suffering of the world. But rarely do we even think of the essential practical application of this truth in the smallest of our pains. Only when the *innocent* part of us begins to suffer is there life and creation within and around us; but for the most part we prefer to remain caught in the vicious and totally unproductive circle of remorse and superficial complacency, followed by a repetition of the sin, more remorse, and so on. In the book of Job, God's condemnation falls on the complacent rationality of the false comforters who assure Job that he could not possibly be suffering unless he were morally guilty. To Job, suffering but innocent, God's answer is simply to reveal himself in his infinite power and glory, beyond rational explanation.

In these days when the media bring to us daily the sight and sound of the appalling sufferings of the innocent, we all have great need of reminders of the only way in which we can contribute to the healing of the terrible split between curse and blessing in our time.

The poets and great storytellers of all ages come to our aid. When one man takes up responsibility for his blindness without any false guilt, even in the smallest things, the self-pity and the projections of blame onto others or onto God drop away, and the blessing beyond the opposites is strengthened in our environment. It seems infinitesimal, but in Jung's words it may be the "makeweight that tips the scales." Thus we suffer the sword of objectivity, refusing nothing, so that the healing may reach "the hearts of many" without our conscious intention. It happens not through our willed efforts to improve the world, fine and right though these may be on another level, but to the degree to which the curse and the blessing have been experienced consciously as one in the psyche of the individual. It is an experience which, as C. G. Jung wrote in *Mysterium Conjunctionis*, reaches "the individual in stillness—the individual who constitutes the meaning of the world."

We began by defining a word. We end with another—the word "passion." Derived from the Latin *passio*, meaning suffering, it is used to define the sufferings of Christ. Commonly the word applies to any emotion which goes beyond the bounds of reason, consuming and possessing a man so that he is in a state of "enthusiasm," which, in its original meaning, is the state of being filled with the god, whether the god of anger, of love, or of hate.

When suffering breaks through the small personal context and exposes a man to the pain and darkness of life itself, the way is opened to that ultimate state of passion beyond all the passions of desire. There, being completely empty, as Christ was empty when he cried, "My God, my God, why hast thou forsaken me?" he may finally come to be filled with the wholeness of God himself.

THE MARRIAGE
VOW

I take thee . . . to have and to hold from this day forward, for better or worse, for richer or poorer, in sickness and in health, to love and to cherish, till death us do part . . . and thereto I plight thee my troth." There are few lovelier words in the English language. The man who speaks them with all his heart, standing in the holy place, is pledging himself to more than the personal marriage between himself and his beloved. She carries for him in that moment, consciously or unconsciously, the image of all womanhood—of that which nourishes and gives birth, not only to physical children but to all the values of true relatedness and to the tender understanding of the heart. To the woman in her turn, her man is the symbol, however obscurely felt, of the sword of the Spirit—of the clear shining of the Word in the darkness. So they take this most solemn vow to love this innermost beauty and cherish it, no matter what the cost, as long as life shall last. Many who have no use for the Church and its rituals will find themselves moved at a wedding as their unconscious responds to the deeply buried image. For the two before the altar are more in that moment than simply the "John" or "Mary" whom we know; they are the symbols of the marriage for which all men yearn in their hearts—the I-Thou meeting, the marriage of Heaven and Earth.

The fact of this commitment in a dimension far beyond their ego consciousness does not, of course, mean that their promise to each other in this world is in any way weakened or devalued. On the contrary, they are now pledged to the daily attempt to live as truly as they are able the meaning of the symbol in all their dealings with each other. Each has chosen a partner in their search with whom to bring forth children, both human and spiritual. There is no hope that they will be able "to love and to cherish" each other unless each is prepared to accept his or her own darkness and weakness and to strive for the "holy marriage" within, thus setting the other free to find his or her individual reality. If there is a continual growth of consciousness through the daily abrasions and delights, and through the hard work of maintaining contact with a sense of the symbolic, then indeed they will together grow into maturity of love. Those who do not marry are equally committed to find partners on their way if they are to know love, bringing the symbol to incarnation in all their relationships with others of whatever kind—with their friends, lovers, enemies, or casual acquaintances.

Married people, however, have made a particular choice, and I am not suggesting that they are not bound to stay with that choice in the face of even repeated failure, as long as there is even a small chance that by staying together they may grow into love. If we break vows for any other reason than out of obedience to a more compelling loyalty, then the situation from which we have tried to escape will simply repeat itself in another form. Nevertheless, for thousands of men and women who take the marriage vow in sincerity, the test of daily life through the years makes it plain that the choice they made was conditioned by projections which, as they fade, leave exposed the fact that the two personalities are, or have become, destructive of each other; or perhaps their levels of consciousness are so far apart that their bond is the cause of their drifting further and further away from the true meaning of their vows. These thoughts, of course, have no validity for those couples who never had any motive in their mating except the satisfaction of their immediate desires and ambitions. For them the vow is in any case devoid of significance and whether they keep it conventionally or not is of no ultimate importance except insofar as children are affected.

Divorce does not always mean that a marriage has been a failure. There are some marriages in which, though both partners have been true to their vows, and have grown through the years into a more adult love, a time may yet come when unlived parts of their personalities are striving to become conscious. A situation may then arise in which it becomes obvious that if they remain together these two, who basically love and will always love each other, will regress into sterility and bitterness if they do not have the courage to accept the suffering of parting. Their quest for wholeness may then demand that they ignore the outer laws of church and society in order to be true to the absolutely binding inner vow "to love and to cherish from this time forward." One does not have to be living with a person—or even to see him or her ever again—in order to love and cherish through everything. A conscious acknowledgment of failures, an unshaken devotion to the love that sets free, can turn a divorce into a thing of positive beauty, an experience through which a man or woman may bring out of the suffering a purer love to all future meetings. The divorce is then a sacrificial, not a destructive act, and the original marriage may remain in the deepest sense procreative to the end of life.

It will be said that the promise at the altar includes the words "and forsaking all others keep thee only unto her as long as ye both shall live." The essence of this vow is a commitment to the utmost loyalty and integrity of which a human being is capable. It is a statement that a man's physical actions are as much a symbol of the singleness of the holy marriage within as any other part of him. In our state of partial consciousness, however, it may and does come about that the man or woman chosen no longer carries the symbol for the partner in any way at all, so that all love, all creation, is dead between them. Surely then the greater loyalties lie in the conscious acceptance of failure and separation. Thus each is set free to seek once more the realization of inner singleness of heart through new experiences of relationship and sex, through a new marriage, perhaps. "Until death us do part." When the symbol is dead between two people, when there is no communication left except on the level of the ego swinging between the opposites, then, if they cling to the letter of the law, a horrible betrayal of the marriage vow results in the unconscious, where animus and anima struggle to destroy each other. Death has parted them in the most real sense of the word.

Yet the Catholic Church still clings to its undifferentiated attitude to these things, she refuses to her children the opportunity of growth through a second marriage, and clings to the rules without regard for individual truth. I read the other day of the simple and beautiful ritual of divorce in the Orkney Islands long ago before the coming of the courts of law. The couple who had decided to part had to go into a certain church together and then quietly go out of it, one by the north door and one by the south. That was all. It was surely the perfect symbol of a true divorce —a hint of its potentially holy character. The couple returns to the altar before which they made their vow as though to renew it in the moment of their parting. One does not stand before the altar in order to announce that one is deliberately about to commit a sin. That simple ritual is an image through which we can feel the humble acceptance of failure, re-spect for individual responsibility, and the seeking of a blessing on a new attempt.

One of the great arguments against recognizing divorce is always the damage that the broken home brings to the child. If it were possible to assess this kind of damage, it would almost certainly be found that the hurt that is done to a child through the unconscious, when he or she is forced to live with parents in whom love for each other has turned to bitterness, is far worse than that caused by a physical breach. However successful the parents may be at covering up the fight between them, the child will suffer the terrifying consequences through the unconscious and will often carry the unsolved conflicts of his father and mother all his life. Insofar as a divorce really means a new chance for the parents to learn to love and is not just a running away, it can be a great gift to a child. Outer-seeming which is not true to the inner condition is a deadly thing —far worse in its impact on others than forthright, passionate sin.

LEVELS

A vital necessity for any association between persons is the discrimination of the levels of relatedness. In any context, as we know, there can be no true meeting or harmony where there is an unconscious mingling—a fuzzy mixture—instead of a conscious separation between the people, things, or functions which seek to unite. This mingling is equally damaging when it involves a confusion of the various *levels*, whether of our activities or of our relationships.

For a woman especially, since she is so close to nature, there is danger that she may mistake this kind of diffuse mingling for a warm connectedness, and the more she falls into this mistake the stronger becomes the compensating divisive factor in the unconscious, erupting into cutting and destructive opinions, vehemently affirmed by the animus, or into gossip and talk with hidden barbs. It may also breed a rigid adherence to rules or to critical and exclusive judgments. Let not the man, however, think it is easier for him! His refusal to "mingle" in the feminine manner, his immunity from what he deems female nonsensical concern over details, may very easily become a kind of superior isolation which of course sets up an extremely "fuzzy mixture" in his unconscious, so that he spreads a fog of moody imprecision around him. Thus in him, too, the awareness of the relative importance of the different levels of life may be distorted, and the true meaning between them precluded.

What are these different levels of which we need to be particularly aware? First and foremost there is the level of the Self, of the Christ within, by whatever name we call it. Our contact with this reality can only be maintained through our efforts to live the symbolic life. It is the responsibility of each one of us to ensure that in the hours of discussion, whether individually or in a group, we keep this truth in our minds and our hearts so that we do not fall into a mere search for outer or comfortable solutions or into disconnected talk. It takes immense vigilance to see that our meetings, one to one or in groups, do not become a kind of field day for losing touch with the Self.

We come now to another level—the personal contact between individuals. A true friendship doesn't just happen; it must be built and maintained by constant hard work. The mutual attraction on which it is built is merely the promise, not the fulfillment. The work to which a person is committed may limit not only the amount of time but the *kind* of energy which he is at liberty to spend in personal contacts; or the development of his inner life may require of him a greater or lesser degree of involvement, as the case may be.

We must be clear, too, about the levels of friendship itself. In its essence, friendship is the capacity for absolute trust in another *as person*, involving a complete honesty with oneself which is extremely hard to attain. At this level it has nothing to do with like or dislike of another's qualities, with agreement or disagreement, or with frequency of contact. It dies if one covers over the qualities in another which one dislikes or exaggerates the things one likes in him. It is killed by any kind of demand, or by such thoughts as "She will be hurt if I don't do what she wants, so I must consent no matter what other values are involved"; equally damaging is the opposite point of view: "My own values are always more important than his or her feelings." In relationship there are no rules, only basic guiding lines, and each tiny situation must be met as something unknown in which we must seek reality and love through a new effort of discrimination.

To the extent, however, that we have grown into the state of basic trust and integrity which is friendship, the other levels of personal relationship will become real and nourishing—a sharing in varying degrees of ideas, feelings, pain, happiness, sheer fun, with those individuals to whom we feel personally akin. Best of all, in contacts between true friends the most hidden tendencies to projection may be uncovered, as well as our subtle demands to be mothered, and our refusals of responsibility. Thus we may grow from unconscious attraction into love.

A third level of relationship involves a whole group of people. At this level the relationship will be real and nourishing only to the extent that the individuals concerned are connected with the fundamental spontaneity and gaiety of heart which is an essential element in the symbolic life. It is a quality that has nothing to do with the frivolity or escaping which are the polar opposites of too great a restraint. Humor and gaiety are an integral part of *real* seriousness.

We may now begin to see that the discrimination of levels is the very reverse of living our lives in compartments. It is indeed our one hope of wholeness. For what is it in fact to live the symbolic life? It is most definitely not to spend certain hours of the week on the study of symbols and images and then to live the rest of our lives on a nonsymbolic level. This is compartment living. On the contrary, the study will be arid and sterile if we do not very quickly realize that there is no smallest detail of our lives that is not symbolic. This does *not* mean that while we are cooking the dinner or dancing with our friends we solemnly think to ourselves, "Now what is the meaning of this?" This is to miss the point entirely. We live symbolically when each thing that we do or say, think or feel is *whole*—not split into the "fact" and the "meaning," not marred by ulterior motives however lofty, when it simply is in itself, not done or said *because* it is useful or good or whatever. When we are caught in this kind of split attitude, we act always out of one opposite or the other or, worse still, out of the two inextricably mixed, and nothing we do is symbolic or has any real meaning.

We return once more to the paradoxical truth that the symbols which unite the opposites and bring us to the beginnings of this kind of wholeness in our day-to-day lives cannot possibly be born in us until we have learned to separate, to discriminate the different levels of being. The meeting between them which we experience through the uniting power of the symbol is entirely different from the kind of halfway-house attitude —a little bit of this and a little bit of that. If we find ourselves thinking some such thing as "A relationship ought to be both personal and impersonal; therefore I won't let myself love so-and-so personally too much, and I will watch that I don't withdraw too far," we are indeed far from the symbol. But it is possible to glimpse for a moment that love which is personal involvement *and* impersonal detachment, each discriminated with the utmost exactitude and at the same time indissolubly one.

There are also the levels of our most secret individual inner lives at one end of the scale and of the ordinary practical tasks and day-to-day responsibilities at the other. These, too, need to be consciously contained and separated so that there may be a unity between them. If we do not set apart a time for the former, it will spread itself all over the place in an inferior and meaningless way, turning into pointless daydreams which go on all the time, either consciously or unconsciously, and steal away energy from our conscious tasks.

There is also the very difficult matter of the shifts we must continually make from one level to another, which is something we too seldom attend to consciously. The *rite d'entrée* and the *rite de sortie* were essential needs in primitive societies—a dance to whip up the mood of war, another to end the war fever and make the transition to peaceful pursuits, a time alone before initiation, and so on. Every individual still needs to find his own "rites," so that he may clearly emerge from one level and enter another. A cup of coffee, listening to music, a brief walk, or, best of all, a few minutes of complete relaxation, are some of the ways we may find. The important thing is to do them consciously; even a few seconds of objective awareness that we are passing from one kind of activity to another is often enough. A great many of our mixed-up approaches to whatever we may be doing, resulting, as they often do, in misunderstandings and resentments, are due in large measure to the fact that we jump from one level to another without so much as drawing breath, so that we never completely let go of one level and never completely enter the other—or are already jumping over the present into concern about future tasks, a condition producing exhaustion, if nothing worse. I do not think the importance of such pauses can be exaggerated. I am reminded of a beautiful sentence from an Indian Tantra which is thought to be as much as five thousand years old. It says, "When in worldly activity, keep attentive between the two breaths (the in breath and the out breath), and so practicing, in a few days be born anew." Well! We can perhaps make a start by attending for a moment between two levels of our multifarious activities.

To the extent, then, that we achieve this discrimination, this attention, our lives are freed from a sense of rush and begin to resemble the pattern of a dance instead of a wild plunging about, each movement clear and whole in itself yet related to all the others in the totality of the great pattern. This is the symbolic life. As Irene de Castillejo has said, in her book *Knowing Woman*, this end may seem very remote but all that matters is that we move toward it. Somehow in each tiny effort the whole is already there if we could but recognize it. Julian of Norwich in her *Revelations of Divine Love* affirmed that no one can seek God who has not already found him.

THE SENSE
OF HUMOR

It is impossible to define that which we call "a sense of humor." Yet perhaps by playing around it in the imagination we may bring to light a little of the wonder, the mystery, of that divine and human gift. Barbara Hannah wrote of C. G. Jung that he often used to quote Schopenhauer, who said, "A sense of humor is the only divine quality of man."

"Humor" itself is a word of many meanings. In the Middle Ages and through the Renaissance it meant, among other things, one of the four principal body fluids that determined human dispositions and health (sanguine, phlegmatic, choleric, melancholic); and in physiology it still means "any clear or hyaline [transparent] body fluid such as blood, lymph or bile." Some other definitions in the American Heritage Dictionary are: "the quality of being laughable or comical"; "a state of mind, mood, spirit"; "a sudden unanticipated whim." The root of the word is the Latin *umor* meaning liquid, fluid. Humor, therefore, on all levels is something that flows, resembling water itself, and symbolizes the movement of unconscious forces gradually evolving into basic characteristics of the individual human being, which express themselves in the body, in moods and emotional reactions, in qualities of feeling, of mind, and of spirit.

The *sense* of humor, however, has a far more elusive meaning. The

American Heritage Dictionary, in defining "sense," after mentioning the five senses we share with the animals, continues, "Intuitive or acquired perception or ability to estimate (a sense of timing). A capacity to appreciate or understand (a sense of humor). Recognition or perception either through the senses or the intellect (a sense of guilt)."

Our humors, therefore, are unconscious drives or reactions, but without consciousness there can be no *sense* of humor at all, however much we may enjoy jokes and absurdities. It is especially interesting that the kind of sense or perception defined as a capacity "to appreciate and understand" is illustrated by a reference to "a sense of humor." The other definitions speak of the senses or the intellect or intuition; only "appreciation and understanding" are words that bring the heart into the matter. This may be a hint to us that the wisdom and compassion of the understanding heart are indeed the core of the laughter that is born from the mature sense of humor.

Most people do not think about the essential difference between a sense of humor and mere reactions to any kind of comical situation. All such things *may* induce laughter whether we have a real sense of humor or not. But the quality of the laughter is very different in those who "appreciate and understand." Those without that kind of perception do not penetrate to the "laughter at the heart of things" of which T. S. Eliot spoke in his introduction to Charles Williams's last novel, *All Hallows Eve.*

Eliot writes of Williams's stories that even for people who never read a novel more than once they are good entertainment, and continues:

> *I believe that is how Williams himself would like them to be read, the first time; for he was a gay and simple man with a keen sense of entertainment and drollery. The deeper things are there just because they belonged to the world he lived in and he could not have kept them out. For the reader who can appreciate them there are terrors in the pit of darkness into which he can make us look; but in the end, we are brought nearer to what another modern explorer of the darkness has called "the laughter at the heart of things."*

Eliot does not name that other modern explorer, but his words express a fundamental truth about those people of whom we can truly say that they possess and communicate a sense of humor. Unless a man or woman has experienced the darkness of the soul, he or she can know nothing of that transforming laughter without which no hint of the ultimate unity of opposites can be faintly intuited.

In all the greatest poets, mystics, and storytellers this sense of humor shines, even when not expressed recognizably in words and images that inspire laughter—even when they are conveying tragedy and sorrow and the darkest experiences of human life. For a very little consideration will show us clearly that the sense of humor is always born of a *sense of proportion*, both in the inner world and in the outer. The sense or perception of proportion means the capacity to discriminate and respond to (to "understand and appreciate") the relationship of the parts of anything to the whole. "Proportion is the desirable, correct or perfect relationship of parts within a whole," according to the American Heritage Dictionary. If we come to the point of retaining a sense of proportion in the midst of all the smallest as well as in the most profound of human emotions, we shall also discover that at the center of every experience is that laughter of God which Meister Eckhart, among many, affirmed with such delight.

There are so many kinds of laughter, and often it conceals a bitterly destructive rejection or contempt. When we yield to that, we are cut off altogether from the sense of humor which always strengthens the compassion in which all our pains and joys become whole. Hurt vanity, our own or another's, personal resentments or anger, humiliations or demands for some change in another—the antics of our alternately inflated or deflated egos—can be accepted with pain and known also as occasions for the laughter that heals. In this laughter we recognize them at once as a temporary loss of "relationship to the whole," to the center that is everywhere. Charles Williams has a wonderful phrase, "the excellent absurdity," referring to any achievement of leadership or power. A man's fate, the meaning of his individual life on earth, is simply to live fully his own particular small part in the pattern of the whole, whether seemingly great or seemingly most ordinary, retaining always that blessed sense of humor about its importance to ourselves or to others with at least the "intention of Joy" (another Williams phrase) even in the midst of emotional pain.

Humility is without question closely related to the sense of humor. The one surely cannot exist without the other. T. S. Eliot, writing about Charles Williams in the introduction to *All Hallows Eve*, states:

> *He appeared completely at ease in surroundings . . . which had intimidated many; and at the same time was modest and unassuming to the point of humility: that unconscious humility, one discovered later, was in him a natural quality, one he possessed to a degree which made one, in time, feel very humble oneself in his presence. . . .*

Eliot is expressing here the identity of a sense of humor with the sense of *proportion* and the humility which this engenders.

C. G. Jung was another, and one of the greatest, explorers of the darkness in this century. He consciously entered the "pit of darkness" in the unconscious and, evading no fact of evil and its horrors, found also the "laughter at the heart of things." Many who knew him well have testified to the quality of his sense of humor and of his laughter, and Laurens van der Post in his biography of Jung wrote a beautiful tribute. He compared Jung's laughter to the laughter of the Bushmen of Africa, thus linking it to the instinctive gaiety of the natural man, of the child, who has not lost his original unity with nature. (Williams also spoke of this gaiety in *The Greater Trumps* as an intrinsic attribute of natural intelligence.) But this natural laughter must surely die when the growth of ego consciousness plunges the individual into the terrible conflicts of the human condition before it is given back at the birth of joy. In between lies "the ethical phase—endurance and action," as Jung once expressed it in a letter. This is the phase of exploration, of purgatorial choices and confrontations, in which we learn to behave "as if" we knew joy without ever disguising to ourselves the actual state of our emotions: then, sooner or later, the true gift of that laughter will come to us, when we least expect it, through the response to life which is a sense of humor —the realization of proportion.

The original gaiety of the natural man had certainly undergone a

night-sea journey in Jung as it must in everyone seeking conscious wholeness. The adolescent ego must go through the struggle to establish its
identity as separate from parents and the environment—a process often
prolonged throughout a lifetime. In this inner struggle we are frequently
caught in a sense of the earthshaking importance of our achievements,
which is a normal phase in the young. But the individual may tragically
remain into adult years obsessed with his or her superiority or inferiority
as the case may be. Nothing more quickly kills the ability to laugh at
oneself which is the sure mark of a sense of humor. We are then left with
the sterile moralities of convention, a kind of solemn and possessive
pursuit of "spirituality" from which the wind that "bloweth where it
listeth" and its laughter are entirely absent. The opposites of these moralities—senseless rebellion, violence, license, greed, and corruption—can
never be controlled by such attitudes. Only the far more difficult search
for the ethics of individual freedom and joy can avail in our predicament.

A sense of humor is in fact the royal road to this freedom and this joy.
One who has it is always ready to laugh at all the pretensions of the ego
in him or herself or in another. This at once differentiates it from intellectual wit and superficial joking and, still more obviously, from the
forced cheerfulness of some who are determined always to do "good," to
improve the ego and the world.

Without this kind of humor no one can experience the laughter of
the reborn child within, for it brings with it a recognition of the fundamental validity of the "other," of object and subject as one. People who
lack this perception may laugh in the same situations, but there is a
subtle difference in their laughter, for it does not spring from the heart
and the belly; at its worst it often contains hidden barbs directed at
another, since it is a protective armor for a frightened ego. We all laugh
at the foibles of those around us, but those with a sense of humor do not
laugh *at* a person; there is simply a feeling of delight in the ridiculous
wherever it is manifest, and such laughter does not condemn the other or
oneself but simply enjoys the sudden recognition of the loss of proportion
in all our human conflicts and contradictions. It is a healing, not a
destructive thing—a delight in life, in its comedies and tragedies, its

seriousness and absurdities—the "excellent absurdities" that Williams loved.

"There are many ways of laughing," wrote Van der Post of Jung's laugh, "but the greatest is that which comes from the joy of seeing disproportion restored to proportion. His laughter was delight, sheer and uncompromising, in the triumph of the significance of the small over the unreality of excess and disproportion in the established great, and so pure a rejoicing in another enlargement, however minute, of the dominion of proportion." And proportion is, once more, "the perfect relationship of the parts to the whole."

It is a sad, even a dangerous loss to Christianity that the gospels and so many of their interpreters never convey the sense of humor that Jesus must certainly have manifested in his life, and we are told nothing of the laughter that must have been so often heard from him and with him. But if one listens imaginatively to some of the stories and sayings it is clearly to be heard. After his ultimate exploration of darkness and the "descent into Hell," it ripples and flows with such joy in the Resurrection stories that the absence of specific references to it cannot hide it. When in later centuries the lives of saints and sages have been described, how often their laughter lifts our hearts. St. Teresa's autobiography, for instance, dances with it.

There is, in fact, no real "spirituality" (a much misunderstood term in these days) without the laughter which the sense of humor brings. It is not to be confused with frivolity and it cannot exist in anyone who is not a serious person able to explore the darkness and suffering in life. The lack of this quality in the soul may also reveal itself among those who seek to lighten the solemnity of their religious beliefs by *mixing* the funny and the serious, making jokes either silly or embarrassing, *about* the deep realities. The sense of humor, the laughter of the Self, never *mixes* things in that way, thus destroying both the serious and the gay. It simply begets in men and women a true perception of all the suffering and the joy, the tears and laughter, the seriousness and the fun, inherent in our experience. When all these opposites are clearly discriminated, they may then be known as one in the unity of the laughter and the tragic darkness of being.

In her diaries Etty Hillesum, a young Dutch Jewish woman, writing during the occupation of Holland by the Nazis, told of the horrible suffering of those who, including herself, were waiting in a camp for transportation to Auschwitz (where she was to die). Her compassion, not only for the victims but for the Germans who inflicted the suffering, shines out from the book, but most moving of all are her words in the midst of the horrors, about her experience of the deepest and most radiant inner joy she had ever known. She tells how she realized what a very little thing all this misery was in the glorious wholeness of the universe. Her joy was the dawning of the sense of proportion, the relationship of every part, however dark, to the whole.

As we wonder how we could possibly have endured such a fate, we are nevertheless inspired by these great ones urgently to seek in our everyday lives a fuller realization of this joy, this laughter. The humdrum tasks, the endless repetitions of the daily round, are often much more difficult to recognize as occasions for this kind of vivid living in the moment than are the more dramatic events of our lives. We hurry through the so-called boring things in order to attend to that which we deem more important and interesting. Perhaps the final freedom will be a recognition that every thing in every moment is *"essential"* and that nothing at all is *"important"*!

The first step on this way is to learn all over again that natural gift of the small child—the gift of "play," which is so conspicuously absent from our society. The natural gaiety and laughter of the child within us is lost in exact proportion to the loss of our ability to play; and it is fascinating to remember the many contexts in which that word is used. We use it unconsciously without any thought of its fundamental meaning and therefore the word often loses its connection with that natural joy. Every kind of dramatic performance is called a play, and all actors are players, as are all musicians, and all ball and game players. Tragedy, comedy, farce, and all kinds of music—Bach, plainsong, jazz, or rock and roll—are brought to us by players, among whom there are those who appreciate and understand the nature of play and so convey the joy of it to their audiences through their "playing" whether of dark truths or light. But there are so many who have no perception of the meaning of play and whose striving motives are to acquire fame and money or self-satisfaction by sensational performances, often in productions without meaning—the opposite of play.

It is even more obvious in sports—which carry for so many the spirit of true play—but which in our day are becoming swallowed up in the atmosphere of big business. The players are, of course, truly playing when they put out all their skill and strength to win, thus reflecting archetypal conflicts. And there still remains in many great individual players and coaches the recognition that without the experience of defeat as well as the exhilaration of victory there can be no real meaning in play. But victory at all costs—secret drugging, violence, corruption, and greed—threatens all sports, and indeed all our activities that cease to be games but become competition for the satisfaction of any kind of demand of the ego. The enormous popularity of sports is a symptom of the deep yearning in all of us for the spirit of play. Through the enjoyment of such things we may discover at last that until our whole lives, whether working or at leisure, are infused by the joy and laughter of play for its own sake—never for the sake of gain—we are not truly alive at all. Work and play would then no longer be opposed to each other but at one in all the different aspects of our lives. Schiller said (again as quoted by Jung), "Man is only fully human when he is at play."

We may begin to intuit the nature of true play if we listen and listen again to the words of Sophia, the holy wisdom of the feminine in the Godhead. They are written in the book of Wisdom (8:22–25) (and they are also in the epistle for the celebration of the birth of Mary the mother of God, in the Roman Catholic liturgy). Without this wisdom of Sophia there can be no Mary within us, women or men, to give birth to the divine, incarnate Child. The translation is from the Douai Bible:

> The Lord possessed me from the beginning of his ways, before he made anything from the beginning. I was set up from eternity, and of old, before the earth was made. . . . I was with him forming all things and was delighted every day, playing before him at all times, playing in the world; and my delight is to be with the children of men. Now, therefore, ye children, hear me. Blessed are they that keep my ways. Hear instruc-

tion and be wise and refuse it not. Blessed is the man that heareth me, and that watcheth daily at my gates and waiteth at the posts of my doors. He that shall find me shall find life, and shall have salvation from the Lord.

When Christ said, "Whosoever shall not receive the kingdom of God as a little child, he shall not enter therein" (Mark 10:15) he was speaking out of this feminine divine wisdom, affirming that beyond the essential "ethical phase," to use Jung's phrase, and beyond all the splendor and beauty of theology, of philosophy, of psychology and scientific research, beyond all the efforts of mankind to understand good and evil, matter and spirit, there still remains a gate through which we must pass if we are to find the ultimate freedom of "the Kingdom of Heaven." It is the gateway to the spontaneous play, not childish but childlike, of the feminine spirit. Without it there never could have been and cannot ever be any creation that knows eternity again after the long journey of Return in the dimension of time. She is and always has been "playing in the world" in the sheer delight of the Fool and the Child hidden in every one of us. As we wait "at the posts of her doors" she may reveal herself to us: then indeed all work is transformed into play and play becomes the work that is contemplation, and we know the delight of being with the sons (and daughters) of men.

I was in the process of writing the above when, synchronistically, I received notice of a seminar to be given by Adolf Guggenbuhl-Craig in New York on "Aging." In the summary of his theme it is said that he suggests it is time to see aging as a process of becoming free . . . "the real archetypal image, the stimulating symbol for the aging would be, not the wise old man or woman, but the 'foolish' old man or woman," then they would find freedom from all conventions and will not care if they show their deficiencies. They would be able to let go of all need to be wise and to do the right thing; they could admit now that they don't understand the world anymore. The archetype would be more accurately described as the Fool and the Child within us rather than as "foolish." The freedom of the Fool and the Child is never silly: it is Sophia "playing in the world."

English literature offers a number of characters who awaken in us that kind of laughter which is beyond all analysis. Through these images we experience the wonder of that sense of humor which, breaking through the bonds of cause-and-effect thinking and superficial morality, touches the innocence of the Fool and the Child in us and brings with it compassion and love.

In Dickens's novel *Dombey and Son*, who can ever forget Mr. Toots? In our day he would have been labeled with some of those empty collective words—"handicapped," "retarded," "brain-damaged," etc.—and treated accordingly, but even today one feels he would have transcended all that. There are many comic characters in Dickens—some great like Toots; others, like Captain Cuttle in the same novel, are mildly funny, though somewhat boring, and do not awaken that fundamental laughter at all. Why? Because Mr. Toots and his peers are wholly themselves, as a small child is wholly him- or herself, and have at the same time a strange kind of natural wisdom that cannot be defined. Mr. Toots, as G. K. Chesterton so beautifully said of him, "always got all the outside things wrong, but all the inside things right." His natural emotions were wholly involved in what he did and felt, but he always assured everyone that it was "of no consequence," as indeed he knew in the humility of his extraordinarily accurate sense of proportion. Susan Nipper, whom he eventually married, said of him, "Immediately I see that innocent in the hall I burst out laughing first and then I choked."

The second immortal image whom one hardly dares approach is Shakespeare's Sir John Falstaff. How can one speak of the essential innocence of the Fool in that fat, drunken, cowardly thief and deceiver? Yet it is there, miraculously there; and he inspires so much true laughter, so much love and delight—both among those who have been most injured by him in the play and in all those blessed with a true sense of humor who read and reread his story—that again we are left with a vision of wonder and delight beyond that final gateway into freedom. This miracle is of course absent from the Falstaff of *The Merry Wives of Windsor*, who is primarily a figure of farce: we may laugh at this Falstaff but we cannot love him. In *Henry IV* and *Henry V*, however, that kind of laughter disappears. To judge his deplorable qualities would be to miss the point absolutely: he is as he is and retains that extraordinary divine quality through it all. He truly loves "sack," as he truly loves life: "If I had a thousand sons, the first humane principle I would teach them should be to forswear thin potations and to addict themselves to sack." On the rational level, his long paean of praise to "sack" is indeed nonsense, but on Falstaff's lips it is a gorgeous celebration of joy in life. Let us indeed forswear the thin potations that we so often give our souls to drink with dreary solemnity. Falstaff creates laughter of the deepest kind all around him and there is no "why" about it. Even the Chief Justice, most reasonably rebuking him for his outrageous behavior, is unconsciously won over.

We feel the tragedy of his rejection, harsh, however necessary, by the prince, now king, and in *Henry V* we are deeply moved by the account of his illness and death when he was nursed by Mistress Quickly—the woman whom he had almost ruined financially and who loved him nevertheless. "Nay, sure, he's not in hell: he's in Arthur's bosom, if ever man went to Arthur's bosom. A' made a finer end and went away an it had been any christom child. . . ." (Act 2, Scene 3.) And Bardolph, his much-abused servant, says, "Would I were with him whether in heaven or in hell!" (Act 2, Scene 3.) How splendid a tribute! Laughter and tears come together as we read this scene if we hear it with the same sense of humor in which these two realities are always present.

Early in *Henry IV, Part 2*, Falstaff seems to recognize for a moment his extraordinary vocation as a kind of divine Fool. "The learning of this foolish and compounded clay, man, is not able to invent anything that tends to laughter, more than I invent or is invented on me: I am not only witty in myself, but the cause that wit is in other men." And later he surely has his values straight when, after the young sober Duke John of Lancaster has said pompously, "I, in my condition, shall better speak of you than you deserve," Falstaff says to himself, "I would you had but the wit: 'twere better than your dukedom. Good faith, this same young sober-blooded boy doth not love me, nor a man cannot make him laugh." (Act 4, Scene 3.)

In our own time the voice of Christopher Alexander is being heard by more and more seekers. He has written and is writing of architecture, of building, as a way to the creation of wholeness in the individual and in the community; and he speaks the same truths as do all the other contemplatives through the ages. In a seminar of his on tape one can hear his belly laugh and recognize it as of the same nature as that of Jung and of Charles Williams as described here—of the same nature as that which bubbles up with our tears as we meet and experience characters such as Toots and Falstaff. In *The Timeless Way of Building*, Alexander writes about the long discipline (the ethical phase of the search for self-knowledge) which teaches us "the true relationship between ourselves and our surroundings." We come then at last to the perception which he calls "egoless" and then we may pass through

> the gate which leads you to the state of mind, in which you live so close to your own heart that you no longer need a language (the old discipline). It is utterly ordinary. It is what is in you already. . . . There is no skill required. It is only a question of whether you will allow yourself to be ordinary, and do what comes naturally to you, and what seems most sensible to your heart . . . not to the images which false learning has coated on your mind.

When we will consent to be "utterly ordinary," to be simple instead of wise, then the "humors" will transform into that *sense* of humor which brings sheer delight in that ordinariness, in the joy of what *is*. Then our instinctive emotions, our moods, the "melancholic, choleric, sanguine or phlegmatic humors" will no longer possess us and project themselves around us in the unconscious. These projections always add to the weight that breeds a desperate need to create drama and excitement in the environment through the hidden greed which is a kind of "antiplay." Instead, in that perception of wonder that is the sense of humor, we can begin to play in the freedom and simplicity of the child. No longer will there be any need to strive after anything—especially not after the spiritual—because the spirit itself would be present in each moment. As the old monk, who was the author of *The Cloud of Unknowing* in the fourteenth century, wrote in his other little treatise, *The Book of Privy Counselling*: [After the long work of learning to know your sinfulness] "Stop

thinking about what you are! Know only that you are what you are. . . .
Remember that you possess an innate ability to know *that you are.*"

At this level the East and West with their different languages are at
one. Sri Ramana Maharshi, that most simple and direct of Hindu sages
(1890–1950), whose laughter and compassion reach us through his words
and his silences, once in answering a question said: "There is no greater
mystery than this—that *being* the reality, we seek to gain reality. We
think there is something hiding our reality and that it must be destroyed
before the reality is gained. It is ridiculous. A day will dawn when you
will yourself laugh at your past efforts. That which will be on the day you
laugh is also here and now." This is "the laughter at the heart of things":
this is the Divine Comedy of Being.

THE CAT
ARCHETYPE

What does the cat mean in the psyche of man that she has acquired such a numinous quality? She inspires the most violent reactions in some people—either of attraction or repulsion—and there are not many other creatures which arouse this same kind of irrational emotion; snakes, spiders, rats, and bats come to mind, but the extreme reaction to these is nearly always one of revulsion only, except in the case of a very few passionate snake-lovers. They have one thing in common: they are all creatures of the dark, of the night, and carry the mystery and *mana* of the unknown. The snake is the most powerful of all animal symbols, the incarnation of evil, the Devil, or of light and healing, the Christ ("As Moses lifted up the serpent in the wilderness, even so must the Son of man be lifted up"—John 3:14), and the legends of the cat also have this double nature. Whereas, however, the snake is cold-blooded—cold with the deathly cold of evil, or cold in the utter conscious aloneness of the Cross—the cat is warm-blooded; her symbolism lies in the realm of the instinctive emotions, much nearer to the everyday struggles of our lives. She differs from all the other animals mentioned above in that, while remaining a creature of the night and essentially remote and mysterious, she is also a creature of the day, welcomed into the house, fed by us, warmed by us, but, unless we delude ourselves, never possessed by us.

What are her qualities? She is an image of the enchanting beauty and grace and precision of natural movement and of the "play" instinct. She has the extreme patience and swiftness of the hunter, and her complete power of relaxation is unique among the animals close to man. Above all she is the only domesticated animal which has retained through all the centuries her qualities of wildness and independence. Kipling's *Just So* story of "The Cat That Walked by Himself" profoundly and delightfully expresses this truth. The horse becomes man's willing servant and the dog becomes man's "first friend," but the cat becomes neither servant nor friend, she simply makes a bargain with the woman [note: *woman*]. She will kill mice, she will purr, she will play with the baby, and in return, the woman will feed her and give her a place by the fire, but always and always she retains her right to say, "I am the cat that walks by himself and all creatures are alike to me." And so, as Konrad Lorenz says, even if a cat goes for walks with you, you always know that it is because *she* chooses, not because you wish it. You cannot train her—at best she will acquiesce in your wishes if it suits her. All genuine cat lovers (not the sentimental cat humanizers) respond with a similar detached respect. (See T. S. Eliot's poem "The Ad-dressing of Cats"—an unknown cat must be approached with much form and ceremony, never with the "old fellow" attitude as with a dog!)

The cat, then, represents in the human psyche the beauty and integrity of our warm-blooded instincts in all their wild independence, to which, if we will, we can relate in our homes, in our consciousness, and which, if we respect and feed them, will protect us from the unseen rats and mice in the dark places of the unconscious which nibble away at our souls. She is the bridge between the wildness of the jungle and our consciousness. The cat, like all pure instinct, is amoral, but until we can learn to accept this essential part of our humanity, to see its beauty and terror and accept it without repressing it or distorting it with sentimental names, we can never come to any true morality, never come to the discipline and freedom of a whole man. We shall remain conventionally "good" on the outside and given over to *immorality* in the unconscious. We shall have broken the pact of humanity with the cat, and as we give her no food or warmth or respect she will leave our house, our mice and rats will multiply and her untamed wildness will be rampant in the dark. Of her negative aspects we will talk more later.

Why is the cat more specifically a feminine symbol? All that independence and the hunting instinct might be superficially thought to be masculine qualities. But the aggressiveness of the bull or the roar of the male lion are very different in kind from the softness, the stillness, followed by the pounce, of the cat (and it is the lioness, not the male lion, who generally hunts for food). The gentleness of the cat's soft paw and the sudden claw are truly feminine! On the positive side, the cat's independence can typify for the woman her emotional freedom, if she will refuse to cling to people or illusions, and will refuse to lie to herself. It can also warn her of the potential coldness and fierceness of her instinctual reactions under their soft feminine exterior: to draw strength and healing from them, she must meet them with her human heart, and with the austerity and detachment and lack of sentimentality of the true woman. Then the fierceness of those instincts can become her strength, her claws can be used not to scratch and tear at others or at herself but to destroy the rats in the dark, and her softness can become real warmth and tenderness instead of the fawning and weakness which too often possess her. Then she has accepted and related to the cat within. (In a man, of course, all this relates to his instinctive anima. The cat qualities are manifest in his moods and she is a more remote symbol for him.)

Finally the cat's capacity to see in the dark connects our conscious values to the life of the unconscious. In this aspect she is an image of the instinctive intuition of the woman, the mediumistic Sybil quality, which can either be a dangerous possession by the dark forces or a great gift of insight and sympathy.

In Egypt the name for cat means "to see," and Bast, the cat goddess, was identified with the eyes of Horus, the sky god. Horus had a sun-eye and a moon-eye, which stood for healing and protection. The cat can see in the dark and she was honored in Egypt for the killing of snakes, so Bast brought protection against both natural and supernatural evil. This belief has persisted through the ages and in Scotland there is a saying that when a person is deluded one should "cast the cat over him." In folklore the head of the black cat, when burned to ashes, was believed to heal blindness—the ashes being blown into a person's eyes three times a day. The tail was, however, held to be the most potent healing agent. Rubbing a sty with a cat's tail was common, and the blood from the tail was used for skin troubles. Sometimes a black cat's tail was buried under the doorstep of a house and was supposed to ward off all disease. The cat's tail has the particular meaning of balance, restoration of equilibrium.

It was told that the Devil's mouse had nibbled a hole in a dark corner of Noah's Ark, and the water was about to rush in when God's cat pounced and killed him and God's frog then sat in the hole and blocked it. In Italy there was a story that St. Francis was praying in his hermitage when hundreds of mice from the Devil jumped out of his sleeves and began to nibble at his feet, to eat him up. But God's holy cat appeared in the nick of time, put the mice to flight, killing all of them except two which escaped into a crevice. The descendants of the holy cat, concludes the story, have ever afterward sat motionless beside holes in the wall, waiting to catch those two fugitives!

Mice and rats are carriers of disease. They represent the problem of uncontrollable hordes, the fragmentation of the collective unconscious invading and devouring us unseen. We have great need of the "holy cat." In the personal sphere, there are people who identify with the mouse mentality. They are the "pounced upon," the constantly "victimized," filled with self-disgust and really *wanting* the worst to happen. Others are "pouncers," identified with (not related to) the cat and pouncing on everyone weaker than themselves. The first kind have the destructive cat in their shadow, the second are "mice" underneath their aggression. All of us have a degree of this cat-mouse symbiosis and need to find the holy cat's eye within us to bring things to light.

There are also images of the cat in her negative forms, as the incarnation of evil. It was in the Middle Ages that she became the symbol of destruction instead of healing, and the opposite pole of the archetype came to the fore. The witch cult and the witch hunt arose, we know, in inevitable response to the over-idealization of the feminine, expressed in the sentimentalized worship of the Virgin Mary shorn of her true humanity, and in the extremes of the cult of the "perfect lady" in courtly love. As always, the unconscious threw up the extreme opposite—the woman who was supposed to be totally given over to evil, to have made a pact with the Devil, her will completely possessed by him.

I am indebted to a lecture given some years ago by Patricia Dale-Green at the Guild of Pastoral Psychology, London, for the following legends. She spoke of the pact of the witch and pointed out that the most coveted gift of the Devil was the power of *revenge*. To implement her revenge, the witch would transform herself into a black cat, but more often she used a real cat as an instrument—her cat-familiar. This was a cat she had bound to her by feeding it with her own blood or with milk from her own breasts—thus establishing an unbreakable identification with the animal. As the witch was bound to the Devil (who himself often appeared as a black cat) by sexual intercourse with him, the "coldness" of his seed breeding hatred and insatiable passion for revenge, so the true animal cat was bound to her and made to serve her evil will, thus destroying that basic freedom of the natural cat of which we have spoken.

All this may seem remote from us, but it is more common than we are easily willing to admit. Insofar as we refuse to see our shadow side, covering it over with sugary so-called "goodness" and conventional facades, evading the starkness of true fact, we constellate the "witch" in the unconscious. If we will not accept and suffer the pain of becoming aware of our natural desires and instincts and of relating to them, consciously and with respect, then the witch inside us will, in the words of the lecture, "fly off in black fantasies on the back of the black cat," and, unseen, we will be possessed by the desire for revenge, and will act under compulsion, completely at the mercy of the instinct which we repress and hold in contempt.

It is surely through this desire for revenge that we can spot the hidden workings of the witch in us. Whenever we find ourselves violently blaming circumstances, other people, bad luck, etc., for our troubles and failures, then we are *avenging* ourselves for the pain of facts, usually facts about ourselves. The claws of the cat are out underneath, no matter how sweet our exterior, and they will be tearing and rending at people around us or at our own souls. The more unconscious this process is the more deadly. The witch, unrecognized, casts spells with the greatest ease. We are now "playing" in the vicious sense with our victims—not playing blamelessly as nature plays, but letting the cat instinct possess us and drown out all humanity. The moment we *use* the cat, use any instinct for personal power or for indulgence of *cold-hearted* intercourse, psychological or physical, then in binding her to us we are delivered over to her unbridled cruelty. If she is not free, she is deadly, her beauty destroyed, her healing night vision turned into the uncanny ability to sense the weak spots in others and use them for her own ends or for the mere pleasure of hurting. These things must be stated in this extreme way if we are to watch for the little things that start up such a process, the little hole made by one mouse, which could end by destroying the whole ark (the totality of life on the earth, in the legend). Our cat, if she is free, will come quickly to the rescue.

There are concrete ways to invoke the help of our "cat." In times when we feel invaded by vague depressions or tensions it is literally as though a hole has been nibbled in our psyche by a mouse out of sight in the dark, and if we will then be very still and allow ourselves to be flooded by whatever emotional reaction is uppermost at that moment— whether of fear, resentment, desire, jealousy, love, or hate—plunging right into it without the censorship of guilt or shame, we will very often find that, on emerging, that little hole has been plugged. The cat has put the mouse to flight. We have set free our emotion (our cat) to be what it is and immediately we are able to see it in its true perspective, to relate it to all our other conscious values, and our energy will flow out into life again. It should be emphasized that such an experience must be given *form*—written, or painted, exactly as it came to us—so it is contained, and we relate to it and are freed from its domination.

There is one more interesting story Dale-Green told which illustrates another aspect of the cat symbol. It concerns the cat vampire, which figures largely in both European and Eastern folklore. A Japanese legend tells of a prince whose concubine was one night killed and buried by a huge cat, which then assumed her form. The prince, knowing nothing of this, continued to make love to the disguised demon, and day by day he grew weaker and weaker as the cat vampire drained his strength away. Servants watched with him at night to try and discover the cause of this but always they were overcome by sleep, until one young soldier asked to be allowed to sit with him. This man, when he began to be drowsy, thrust a dagger into his own thigh to keep himself awake and succeeded in discovering the vampire. His gaze was enough to render her powerless, so she turned back into a cat and escaped to the mountains. The prince quickly recovered.

Here is a picture of the possession of man's anima, or feminine side, by the cat. The man is then completely at the mercy of every mood and has a sense of being drained of all energy. We all know, too, how some people, whose unconscious is in the grip of a destructive attitude, can drain away the strength of those around them. Their negativity feeds on our creative energy. Psychic exhaustion comes always from some degree of "vampire" possession, which sucks our lifeblood, delivering us over to the forces which fight to destroy consciousness. It is only when we are "asleep" that this can happen. When we are ready and willing to suffer acute pain, as did the soldier in the story, in the effort to stay awake, to be constantly aware, then the spell is broken and we are free.

Ghosts and vampires are unconscious contents which we have "killed," totally rejected, or, alternatively, attitudes which we have in truth outgrown, but which we refuse to bury. They are dead but we still cling to the corpses and so are haunted, drained of blood. The horror of all primitives of an unburied corpse is well founded in psychic reality— the ghost then walks and saps our life.

As Dale-Green concluded, "The power of the sacred eye of the Cat Goddess is stronger than that of the evil eye of the witch. The witch-cat may poison people's minds, infect their bodies and inflict both with blindness, but the Cat Goddess is a destroyer of poison, a healer of blindness, and a bringer of good health."

PART

III

THE INNER STORY

The essence of all religions, from the most primitive to the most highly developed, has always been expressed by the human soul in stories. The Mass itself is a story—a symbolic drama telling the great story of the death and resurrection of Christ. We can say, "I believe in this or that," and assert the truth of many doctrines, but these things will not affect the soul of any one of us unless in some way we experience their meaning through intense response to the images conveyed in story. Innumerable tales in all ages have expressed the changing relationships of human beings to their gods and have told of their search for the divine meaning behind their lives.

Before the invention of writing all human knowledge was conveyed from generation to generation by storytellers who were the sacred minstrels and medicine men of the people; and, even after the growth of consciousness had brought about the formulation of doctrines and the definitions of dogma, the great storytellers kept alive into our own day the imaginative response to the numinous, which alone gives life to conceptual dogma.

Many theologians and psychologists nowadays are joining poets in affirming anew the tremendous importance of story. A friend who is a theologian was saying to me the other day that, valuable as conceptual theory is, it can only speak to the intellectual faculties in men and women; whereas in a story the living confrontation of the opposites and the transcendent symbol that resolves conflict speak directly to the listener's mind, heart, and imagination in the same images.

C. G. Jung has told us how he found, after his own lonely confrontation with the powers of the unconscious, the life-giving wonder of the inner myth, or story, behind his life; and it is in part by our response to the great stories of the world that we too can begin to find, each of us, this individual story, expressing the symbolic meaning behind the facts of our fate and behind the motives that determine the day-to-day choices of our lives. If we are not aware of the need for this imaginative search, and continue to base our attitudes purely on the kind of thinking that is bounded by the laws of materialistic cause and effect and statistical data, then sooner or later we shall be forced to see how the springs of life dry up, and how nature, physical as well as psychic, is gradually polluted and sterilized, so that we look forward to a time when there will be no pure water left for us to drink. Yet there is a steadily growing hope in the increasing number of people who drink from the life-giving springs of the images within. Many of my writings are simply a collection of studies made with small groups over the years, as we looked at some of the great stories, ancient and modern, and sought to realize their meaning in our lives.

The experience of darkness, of evil, is essential to redemption and there is no inner story that does not contain this truth. As Judas and the Pharisees were essential to Christ's death and resurrection, so in every story of the soul the tiny flame of love and awareness is threatened with extinction, and saved only through the humility and sacrifice of an individual human being.

At the end of his life C. G. Jung (as we can see in his later letters) continually stressed that *only* if enough individuals would commit themselves totally to this search, each for his or her own inner truth, could the world avoid disaster. The inner story, though the same in essence for all, is always single and unique in each human being, never before lived and never to be repeated.

AN AFRICAN TALE

A real story touches not only the mind but also the imagination and the unconscious depths in a person, and it may remain with him or her through many years, coming to the surface of consciousness now and then to yield new insights. A great teacher of English at Swarthmore College, the late Harold Goddard, wrote in his book *The Meaning of Shakespeare*, "The destiny of the world is determined less by the battles that are lost and won than by the stories it loves and believes in." This love and belief begins and ends, of course, in individuals and their responses to such stories in their own lives. I heard the following story a number of years ago told by Laurens van der Post at a conference. He had heard it from a Zulu wise man in Africa, and he was retelling it as an offering of gratitude and respect to the women of the world.

All those stories that deal with basic human themes draw their power from the archetypal world that is common to people of all cultures and of all times, but the images in each culture will, of course, differ greatly, and it is for us to penetrate through these varying pictures to the universal wisdom that underlies them. I propose to tell the story first, simply, as it is told in its African context; and afterward I will go through it again with a few indications as to how it may yield its wisdom in terms of our own lives. It is a story about young women on the threshold of their adult lives—and that is a rare thing to find. There is no hero in it at all—only one somewhat devastating male figure!

In an African village a group of young women had banded together to humiliate one of their number of whom they were jealous and whom they had rejected because she was "different," and especially because it seemed to them that she had a necklace of beads that was more beautiful than their necklaces.

These jealous young women ran down to the banks of the river and there they planned a trap for the envied one. When she joined them they told her that they had all thrown their necklaces into the river as an offering to the river god. The young woman was a person of generous heart, so she at once took off her own necklace and threw it into the river; whereupon the others dug up their necklaces, which they had buried in the sand, and went off laughing and sneering.

The young woman, left alone, was very sad. She had been duped into a well-meant but foolish act, and she wandered along the riverbank, praying to the god to restore the necklace. There was no answer until at last she heard a voice, bidding her plunge into a deep pool nearby. She did not hesitate, for she knew it was the voice of the god. She plunged down into the unknown and found herself on the riverbed, where an old woman sat waiting. This old one was exceedingly ugly, even repulsive, for she was covered with open sores, and she spoke to the girl, saying, "Lick my sores!" At once the girl obeyed out of her compassionate heart, and licked the repulsive sores as she had been asked to do. Then the old woman said to her, "Because you have not held back and have licked my sores, I will hide and protect you when the demon comes who devours the flesh of young women." At that she heard a roar and a huge male monster came, calling out that he smelled a maiden there. But the old woman had hidden her away, and soon he went off cursing.

Then the old woman said to the girl, "Here is your necklace"—and she put around her neck beads of far greater beauty than any she had had before. "Go back now," the old woman said, "to your village, but when you have gone a few yards from the pool, you will see a stone in the path. Pick up this rock and throw it back into the pool. Then go on without looking back and take up your ordinary life in your village."

The young woman obeyed. She found the stone and threw it back and came to the village without a backward look. There the other girls quickly noticed her beautiful new necklace and clamored to know where she had found it—to which she replied that it had been given to her by the old woman at the bottom of the pool in the river. Not waiting for more, they all rushed off in a body and jumped into the pool. And the old woman said to each of them as she had said before, "Lick my sores!" but these girls all laughed at her and said they wouldn't dream of doing anything so repulsive—and useless, too—and they demanded to be given necklaces at once. In the midst of all this there came the roar of the giant demon, who seized upon those girls, one after the other, and made a mighty meal of them. And with that the story comes to an end.

I shall now look briefly at the images in the story as symbols of certain attitudes, conscious or unconscious, that are alive in each one of us and influence us in often unrealized and subtle ways. Stories like this are not manufactured by the intellect; they are the symbolic dreams of humanity.

The necklace in Africa is a highly prized symbol of a woman's identity and worth as a person. The group of girls in the story play a particularly unkind trick since it concerns devotion to a divine, transpersonal value. It is the product of group mentality, mass thinking, which so often covers and excuses hatred and cruelty. This is perhaps the worst menace in our society, requiring great effort and integrity to resist.

Notice the ease with which the simple girl falls into the trap. This is surely a warning of the dangers that lie in wait for the generous-hearted, who are so quickly induced by the slogans of some cause or crusade, fine in itself perhaps, and sponsored by people we long to please. We lose sight of our individual responsibility to reflect and to *choose*, and thus, as it were, we throw away our identity. Nevertheless, the story goes on to show us that such naive enthusiasms, *if* they truly involve the intention of a personal sacrifice to that which is greater than our egos, to the river of life itself, may indeed bring about the shock that leads us out of group thinking to the discovery of our meaning as individuals on a much deeper level.

The young woman in the story had a rude awakening from her identification with her peers. We may notice that she did not waste energy on resentment or remorse. She stayed alone beside the river of life, praying that she might rediscover her value as a person, waiting for an inner voice to bring her wisdom. And it came. She was to look for her necklace down under the water. Only by going *down*, not by striving upward, would she find herself. She must plunge into the river of life *unconditionally*, risking mistakes or failure, not just throwing things, however valuable, into the river. Only by trusting herself to the unknown, both in her outer life and in her own hidden depths, would she find her unique way.

This young woman was now obedient, not to convention or opinions or slogans, but to that voice from within that may be heard by us all at the crucial moments of life, if we will truly listen.

She plunged down into the pool and there she found—not a radiant woman, symbolizing her potential beauty and power, but an old, ugly, repulsive thing with open sores. How shall we read this image for ourselves? When we enter with open eyes into the river of life, we find ourselves face to face with the ugliness, the suffering from which we have perhaps been protected hitherto in many different ways. And it is now that the story yields to us its specifically *feminine* wisdom.

We may take this image of the old woman on two levels. She may stand for the suffering that contempt for the feminine values has brought to all women through the ages—a contempt of which not only many men have been guilty, but also large numbers of women themselves, especially in our time. And secondly, the old woman is an image on the personal level of the most despised and repellent things in our own psyches that we refuse to acknowledge and from which we turn often in disgust.

The old woman's invitation is clear. "You can't bring help to me by any kind of technical, scientific, impersonal and collective panacea, or by *talk about* justice and freedom. Only with your own saliva can you bring healing to these sores in yourself and in the world." Saliva is symbolically a healing water that we are all born with. The licking of an animal is its one means of healing wounds, and we may remember Christ's saliva on the blind man's eyes. So the girl is asked to give of her own unique essence—to bring healing to the sores, not by words out of her mouth but by water from her mouth. Because she is on the threshold of true womanhood the girl at once responds out of that essential core of the feminine being—the compassionate heart. Here I would emphasize that true compassion bears *no* resemblance to a vague and sentimental pity. Compassion is not just an emotion; it is an austere thing and a highly differentiated quality of soul.

And now comes that universal threat—the demon of inferior masculinity that can so easily devour our womanhood. When this happens, we simply lose ourselves in an imitation of men, which kills the truly creative masculine spirit in a woman, and, however outwardly successful she may be, all hope of equality of *value* in the world of men disappears.

Had there been a male "hero" present, we might imagine the old woman telling him to take up his sword and fight the monster of greed and aggression. But to every woman she will always say, "Because of your compassion you will be freed from him."

So it came about that the devouring ambition and greed had no power over the woman who had the courage and humility to lick the repellent sores. It is at this moment that she receives her own individual and unique necklace—she does not just recover the old one that had come from her family before her initiation into life. This necklace is hers and hers alone.

It is time to return to her life in the world, to the daily, ordinary tasks and relationships. In her case, marriage and children awaited her and the building of a home; in our time and place, a career most probably awaits her, with or without the ancient way of woman in the home. But whether she marries and bears children or not, this ancient responsibility of woman remains. She is the guardian of the values of feeling in her environment, and if she remains aware of that compassion, that quiet, hidden nurturing that is the center of her feminine nature, then her skills in any kind of work whatsoever will grow in the manner of trees, well rooted and strong, and her creative spirit will be free. The woman who has received the necklace from the old woman in the pool does not seek compulsively to achieve success after success, collecting necklace after necklace, so to speak. Always she will remember to "lick the sores" and to remain still and hidden when the demon of greedy ambition threatens, whether at home or in the public arena.

Now as to the stone that the girl was to find and throw back, I'll give you one hint and leave you to work it out. The stone in all cultures is the symbol of the immortal Self, and this is the true offering to the divinity in the river. Don't pick it up and put it in your pocket!

The last bit of the story speaks for itself. All those greedy girls who did not bother to reflect on the meaning of life went rushing off in a mob, all wanting more and better necklaces, which in our day would be more and more demands for wealth, or success, or men, or publicity, or security, or even for spiritual experiences. They refused with contempt the essential task of a woman, the compassionate "licking of the sores" in themselves and in their immediate environment. They were therefore devoured by the demon that rages around, assimilating such women to itself.

I believe it was Charles Williams, the English poet and novelist who died in 1945, who once defined the art of living as the ability to live the ordinary in an extraordinary way and to live the extraordinary in an ordinary way. The story illuminates this beautiful saying. Dame Janet Baker, a great singer and a great woman, said once in an interview, "I've found that the ordinary things are the important things. . . . We all—in life and music—have our backs up against the wall trying to preserve order and quality. . . . My gift is God-given and it must be given back. We all have a gift to give, and if you give it with sense of holy obligation everything clicks into place."

Each of us, as we journey through life, has the opportunity to find and to give his or her unique gift. Whether that gift is great or small in the eyes of the world does not matter at all—not at all; it is through the finding and the giving that we may come to know the joy that lies at the center of both the dark times and the light.

MOTHER
AND DAUGHTER
MYSTERIES

There is a story written in this century that speaks with particular power to the predicament of women in our time. C. S. Lewis, toward the end of his life, wrote *Till We Have Faces*—a story based on the myth of Psyche and Eros and told from the point of view of one of the ugly sisters. I mention it here because it is an example of how an old myth grows into contemporary relevance through the imagination of an individual expressing the unconscious need of his or her time.

However, the still more ancient myth of Demeter and Kore is a seedbed of feminine experience for women of all times and places, and I shall now try to explore some of its unchanging wisdom.

The story, taken from the Homeric "Hymn to Demeter," is as follows.

Demeter's lovely daughter Persephone (also called Kore) was playing with her companions in the meadows and, wandering off by herself, she saw a flower, a narcissus with one hundred blossoms, which Zeus himself with help of Gaia, goddess of earth, had caused to grow as a snare for her. Fascinated by this flower, with its intoxicating scent, she reached to pick it. At that moment the earth opened, and the Lord of the Dead himself appeared from the depths with his immortal horses and, seizing her in spite of her cries, carried her off to the underworld, unseen and unheard by any except the goddess Hecate who, as she was thinking "delicate thoughts," heard the cry from her cave. Otherwise only Helios the Sun himself witnessed the act. Persephone cried out to Zeus to save her, but he took no notice at all, for he himself had planned the whole thing.

The mountains and the depths of the sea, however, carried the sound of her voice, and "her lady mother heard her." For nine days the sorrowing mother, the great goddess Demeter, wandered over the earth carrying burning torches and stopping neither to eat nor to wash, but no one anywhere could give her news of her lost daughter.

But on the tenth day came the goddess Hecate, bearing a torch, and told the seeking mother that her daughter had been ravished away, but that she had heard only and not seen who the ravisher might be. Then together the two goddesses went to Helios the Sun as he drove his chariot across the heavens, and Demeter entreated him to tell her what he had seen. He answered that Zeus himself had given Kore to his brother Hades for his wife, and he urged her to cease lamenting as this was a good marriage for her daughter.

But her grief only increased the more and she wandered unknown, and disfigured by sorrow, among the cities of men, until she came one day to Eleusis and there she sat by the wayside beside the Maidens' Well where the women came to draw water. She bore the form of an old woman past childbearing, and she sat in the shade of an olive tree. Then came the four daughters of the king of Eleusis to draw water, and when they saw her they questioned her, and she told them that she was far from her home in Crete and sought for work—to nurse a child perhaps. Then the princesses led her to their father and mother, for they needed a nurse for a late-born son. With her dark robe and her head veiled she came into the house of the king, and her great height and the light which came from her struck awe into them all. At first she sat sad and speechless, but the ribald jokes of an old woman cheered her. When they offered her wine, she refused it saying she was not permitted to drink it and asking for meal and water mixed. Then she took the child from his mother and held him "on her fragrant heart," and he grew daily stronger and more beautiful on food that was more than mortal. Each night she took the child and laid him in the fire like a brand while his parents slept. But one night the child's mother came in the night and saw what was being done to her child and cried out in terror and anger and snatched him from the goddess, thus depriving him of immortality. The goddess revealed her identity, upbraiding the mother for her "witlessness" in destroying the child's chance of immortality, and she ordered that a great temple be built for her there in Eleusis. When this was done she sat within the temple and mourned for her daughter.

Now she brought a terrible year on mankind, for she withheld growth from the earth, and no seed came up, and all the fruits of the earth were withering, so that mankind would surely have perished, and the gods would have been left without worshipers. So now Zeus in his heaven sent Iris to Demeter and begged and implored her to return among the gods and restore fertility to the earth, but she was deaf to all his pleading, even when each and all of the gods had come one by one to persuade her. And then at last Zeus sent Hermes to his brother Hades to tell him he must release Kore to her mother Demeter so that she might no longer withhold the seed from the earth.

Hades then turned to the still grieving Persephone and said that she might go, but offered her a pomegranate seed to eat as they parted. And she, though she had eaten nothing in the underworld, now, in her joy, took it and ate it, thus ensuring that she must return. Only if she had not eaten could she stay always with her mother. Henceforth she must return always to the underworld for one third of the year. Then as they rejoiced in each other Hecate came again and kissed Kore many times and from that day was her "queenly comrade." And then spring burst forth on the earth, but for one third of each year the trees were bare and the land lay fallow. And as Demeter caused the grain to grow rich and fat again, she taught the meaning of it to all the rulers in Eleusis and gave instructions as to her rites and the mysteries which should be celebrated there.

In his essay on the Kore (the primordial maiden) Jung has said, "Demeter and Kore, mother and daughter, extend the feminine consciousness upward and downward—and widen out the narrowly conscious mind bound in space and time, giving it intimations of a greater and more comprehensive personality which has a share in the eternal course of things. . . . It seems clear enough that the man's anima found projection in the Demeter cult. . . . For a man, anima experiences are of immense and abiding significance. But the Demeter-Kore myth is far too feminine to have been merely the result of an anima projection. . . . Demeter-Kore exists on the plane of mother-daughter experience which is alien to man and shuts him out."

There is an immense difference between the mother-son and the mother-daughter experience. On the archetypal level the son carries for the mother the image of her inner quest, but the daughter is the extension of her very self, carrying her back into the past and her own youth and forward to the promise of her own rebirth into a new personality, into the awareness of the Self. In the natural pattern of development the boy will feel his separateness from his mother by reason of his masculinity much sooner than the girl and will begin his striving for achievement. Everywhere, however, before the twentieth century, the growing girl remained at home contained in the orbit of her mother until the time came for her to become a mother herself and so reverse her role. Thus she would grow naturally from the passive state of being protected into the vital passivity of opening herself to receive the seed, the transition point being marked actually or symbolically by the violent breaking of her virginity.

Margaret Mead has written, "If women are to be restless and questing even in face of child-bearing they must be made so through education." For better, for worse, she has been made so. It can lead a woman either to disaster or to her great opportunity, and if she is to succeed in bridging the gap it is vital that, in one way or another, she pass through the Demeter-Kore experience in her inner life.

In ancient Greece the Eleusinian mysteries of Demeter bear witness to this overwhelming need of woman in her already growing separation from the natural pattern of the primitive feminine—the need for the goddess to teach her the *meaning* of the deep transformation of her being from daughter to mother to daughter again. How much greater is that need today, when so often the woman lives almost like a man in the outer world and must find the whole meaning of her motherhood inwardly instead of physically, and when so many of those who do bear children are simply playing at "mothers and babies," never having allowed themselves to experience consciously the violent end of their daughter identification. There is strong evidence that the man initiated into the mysteries also "became" the *goddess*, not the *god*. He too, in the flowering of Athenian civilization and the growing split between the conscious and unconscious, and between reason and the ancient goddesses of the earth and moon, must go through a profound anima experience and rediscover the meaning of the feminine within, must free his infantile anima from possession by the mother, and then find her again as mature and objective feeling, mother and maiden in one.

Persephone is playing with her companions in the eternal spring, completely contained in her carefree belief that nothing can change this happy state of youth and beauty. Underneath, however, the urge to consciousness is stirring, and "the maiden not to be named" strays away from her fellows, and, intoxicated by the scent of a narcissus, she stoops to pick it and in so doing opens the door through which the Lord of the Underworld rushes up to seize her. We may notice here that Gaia, Mother Earth, is clearly distinguished from Demeter in this myth. She is Zeus's fellow conspirator as it were! Carl Kerenyi says, "From the Earth Mother's point of view, neither seduction nor death is the least bit tragic or even dramatic."

It is through the father that the daughter first becomes conscious of her self. When there is no adequate father image in a girl's life, the identity of daughter and mother can assume a tremendous intensity, or else when the father image is very negative and frightening, the daughter may unconsciously take on the mother's problem in a peculiarly deep way, sometimes carrying it all her life, long after the mother's death, and so remaining crippled in her effort to face her own fate in freedom. Normally the girl begins to detach from the mother and to become conscious of her own potential motherhood through love of the father. Thus she is ready for the intoxicating moment of finding the narcissus—seeing *herself* as a person (as Narcissus saw his own face in the water), and the inevitable rape will follow. Dionysos was admiring himself in a mirror when he was set upon by the Titans and torn to pieces, the dismemberment which led to his rebirth. He is a male counterpart of Persephone.

The moment of breakthrough for a woman is always symbolically a rape—a necessity—something which takes hold with overmastering power and brooks no resistance. The arranged marriages of the primitive were often accompanied by a ritual stealing of the woman. The carrying of the woman over the threshold has survived through the centuries, becoming finally a joke, its connection with myth being lost. Any breakthrough of new consciousness, though it may have been maturing for months or years out of sight, comes through a building up of tension which reaches a breaking point. If the man or woman stands firm with courage, the breakdown becomes a breakthrough into a surge of new life. If he cannot stand it and settles for an evasion, then he will regress into neurosis.

The Lord of the Underworld is he who arises, bursts forth from the unconscious with all the tremendous power of instinct. He comes "with his immortal horses" and sweeps the maiden (the anima in a man) from the surface life of her childish paradise into the depths, into the kingdom of the dead—for a woman's total giving of her heart, of herself, in her experience of her instincts is a kind of death. This statement in no way equates this total giving with the outward experience of intercourse with a man. This is a normal part of it and by far the easiest way, but the instincts may be experienced to the full, sometimes perhaps even more profoundly, by a woman whose fate does not bring her the fruition of intercourse on the physical plane. An immature man may experience his instincts in a compartment, so to speak, without deep-seated damage— but not so a woman. If she does so she pays a very great price. It was not merely a man-made piece of injustice that condemned a woman's adultery as so much more shameful than a man's. The horrible cruelty of conventional prejudices should not blind us to the archetypal truths from which these distorted collective judgments spring. The woman who gives herself on the instinctual level without the love of her heart betrays the very essence of her being as woman. A prostitute, so called, whose warmth of *heart* flows out to the man in her every encounter is a far more moral person than the respectable wife who fulfills her "duty" with hidden hatred in her heart.

Persephone cries out in fear and protest as the cord of her tie to her mother, to her unconscious youthfulness, is violently cut, and nearby, Hecate, the goddess of the moon, hears her in her dark cave, though she does not see the abduction. There are three goddesses in the myth, Demeter, Persephone, and Hecate, and they are three aspects of woman. Hecate is the goddess of the dark moon, of the mediumistic intuition in woman of that which *hears* in the dark but does not see or understand. In this myth she appears as beneficent, linked positively to the others, but she has also of course her negative side. Disconnected from the other aspects of woman or from a man's undeveloped feeling, she is the goddess of ghosts and witches and of the spells with which the unconscious binds us, or those near to us, from below. Mother earth and the sea, the mother of all, also carry the sound of the daughter's voice, and Demeter, the mother, hears and knows that the daughter is lost but not how. For nine days she wanders over the earth in fear and sorrow, searching for her daughter but not *understanding*. She is wholly identified with her grief, swallowed by it, even her body forgotten so that she does not eat or wash. It is the beginning of the unspeakably painful struggle of a woman to separate from her possessive emotions, the struggle which alone can give birth to love. As Demeter sank into her grief, so every time we are shocked out of some happy identification with another, which we have fondly imagined to be an unbreakable state, we are beset by the temptation to this surrender, to this despairing search for that which has been lost, demanding that it be restored to us exactly as it was, without any effort to discover the meaning of the experience. If we imagine we have succeeded in restoring the status quo, then the whole story will begin again and repeat itself endlessly and pointlessly until we can follow the goddess to the next step—the dawning of her attempt to *understand*. This cut, this loss, must be experienced by every woman both as daughter and as mother or, especially in later years, as *both* at the same time, for in every relationship between two women the mother and the daughter archetypes are constellated; each may mother the other, each may depend on the other and ask to be mothered—the balance weighted now one way, now the other.

At this point we will look at the specific experience of the loss of the daughter in older women. It is the loss of the young and carefree part of oneself, the opportunity for the discoveries of meaning which are the task of the second half of life: it is the change from the life of outer projection to the detachment, the turning inward, which leads to the "immediate experience of being outside time" in Jung's words. In the language of this myth Death rises up and takes away the woman's belief in everlasting spring. The great majority of women today, having no contact at all with the Demeter mystery, have extreme difficulty in giving up this unconscious clinging to youth, their partial identification with man's anima image, the unraped Persephone eternally picking flowers in blissful unconsciousness of the dark world below her. To such women the menopause brings long-drawn-out disturbances of the body and the psyche as the conflict grows more acute and remains unresolved.

Kerenyi has written, "To enter into the figure of Demeter means to be pursued, to be robbed, to be raped" (as Persephone), "to rage and grieve, to fail to understand" (as Demeter), "and then to get everything back and be born again" (as Demeter and Persephone—the twofold single reality of Demeter-Kore). There can be no short cuts in this experience. All through her nine-day search (the symbolic nine of pregnancy) in her unconscious abandonment to grief the goddess had nevertheless carried burning torches in her hand, symbol perhaps of that small fire of attention which must be kept burning through the darkness of our journey when all meaning seems to have left us. On the tenth day Hecate, the hitherto dormant intuition, comes, also bearing a torch, and tells Demeter that her daughter has been ravished away, though she does not know who the ravisher may be. Demeter's moon nature brings the first rift in the isolation her absorbing personal grief has created. The stricken mother begins to intuit, to hear for the first time a voice which leads her to reflect upon that which has brought about her loss. She emerges enough from her self-concern to seek the aid of conscious reason. Together the two goddesses approach and question Helios the Sun, and he tells Demeter what has happened—that Zeus himself has arranged this marriage for her daughter and that this should be accepted as a good, a happy fate. But although her conscious mind has seen and understood, she cannot accept this reasonable answer. "She fails to understand" with her essential being and continues "to rage and to grieve."

Strangely enough, a woman is certainly right to reject this all too easy rational solution. "Let us be sensible," we say. "Our loss is good for us. Our grief was nothing but a childish reaction," and so on. Nevertheless the sun's calm reasoning has affected us. We must go on living. We must emerge from this totally self-centered, self-pitying sorrow and be awake to other people. We must work, we must relate, but we must not deny our grief. And so Demeter comes to the Well of the Maidens at Eleusis—the place where the woman consciously draws the water up from the depths —and listens to the wisdom of the unconscious. There, sitting under an olive tree, she meets the king's daughters and offers to work as nurse to a child or at any menial task. No longer obsessed with *her* child, she can look again on the beautiful daughters of others and respond.

She goes to the palace. Arrived there, she takes a lowly seat and her royal hosts offer her a cup of wine. But this she refuses and asks for a mixed drink of meal and water. It is not time yet for the wine of new life, the wine of full communion. We may remember here the words of Christ before his Passion. "I will not drink henceforth of the fruit of the vine until that day when I drink it new with you in my Father's kingdom." There is a time when all seeking of release from tension must be refused, and the drink must be plain and tasteless.

The goddess remains deeply sad in her bearing and there follows the delightful image of the first smile appearing on her face as she listens to the crude jokes of Iamba, the serving woman. Her load is not lightened by some lofty thought but by a most earthy kind of humor. The ancients were not cursed with the puritanical split between earth and the holy.

This then is the next step, after a loss, after any emotional blow, even after a seemingly trivial incident involving hurt feelings. We must return to the well of feminine wisdom. We can always work and we can always serve and we can recover our sense of humor, if we will descend far enough from our goddess-like superiority. Demeter here appears as a woman past childbearing—she has lost her own child; she can never bear another in the flesh. Even the partial acceptance of this means that she can now give of her wisdom to the children of others. Demeter, being a goddess, has the power to bestow immortality, and she feeds the child of the king and queen with inner wisdom, and at night she thrusts him like a brand into the fire which burns but does not consume.

What is the meaning of this incident for us? It can perhaps be seen from two opposite angles. The fear and the protest of the human mother are on the one hand warnings of how fatal to a child's inner life is the overprotective possessiveness of mother love which tries to prevent all suffering and danger from touching the beloved son. But from another angle, on another level, the human mother's instinct is surely right. This is a human baby and must grow up into a human being, subject to death. If he is to reach immortality, he must reach it on the hard road of human experience and the battle for consciousness—not be given immunity and deprived of the suffering and dignity of manhood by a goddess. She is right, as a mother's instinct so often is, even if for the wrong reasons. It may be noted that the goddess here descends to something like a temper tantrum, throwing the child heartlessly onto the floor and reviling the mother for her witlessness and for her lack of vision.

It could be that the goddess's behavior at this point gives us a glimpse into another danger of the way. After a violent awakening to loss, inner or outer, when already we have been greatly matured by this, and when we have, perhaps with great courage, decided to do our best to serve and to work, it is often a great temptation to seek assuagement for our anger and grief in the satisfaction of passing on to others who are still in a very unconscious state our hard-won wisdom, and then to get very angry when this priceless gift is refused.

In a woman, it would not be so much a matter of preaching ideas as of being quite sure she can save someone else from having to go through the same agony. To feed the infant the food of divine wisdom is well, but to thrust him into the fire of premature transformation is to deprive him of his choice as a human being. Many women do this when they unconsciously lay on their sons the burden of their own unlived inner quest, thrusting them inexorably into the priesthood or similar "spiritual" vocation at an early age. Of this particular child we are told that all his life long the food of the goddess made him wiser than other men but, thanks to his mother, he remained a man, retained his human fate and his human dignity.

As is the way with myth, this in no way invalidates the other mean-ing—the danger of overprotection. There are very few mothers who do not react as this one did when they see the Great Mother, life itself, thrusting their child—their outer or their inner child—into the fire. Only when she herself will accept the Demeter experience is she strong enough to consent to this. This is why the woman's experience of the dark is so often expressed in myth by the descent of the child, daughter or, more often, son, into Hell. It is a more terrible experience for the feminine psyche than her own descent. The woman does not hang on the cross. She stands at its foot and watches the torment of her son. This is an image expressing the truth that immortality can only be realized through the sacrifice of the most precious thing of all—and that for a woman is her child, whether of the flesh or of the spirit. Christ was the Word incarnate and his life's work was mocked and spurned and came to ignominious failure. Mary was the mother incarnate and her sacrifice was quite simply the complete acceptance of that which happened to her son, which meant the death of every shred of possessiveness. Every archetypal story tells of course of the experience in its pure form. It is the theme upon which the endless variations in the individual psyche are built.

Demeter's effort to transmit immortality to the unconscious child may also be seen as an attempt at a short cut, if we think of the child for a moment as her own new consciousness. After a partial awakening it is easy to imagine that we have already arrived, or that the "baptism of fire" can now take place immediately through some kind of miracle or through self-imposed, dramatic purging—that we won't need to suffer it through in actual experience over the years. Demeter has a long road to travel before she comes to the holy marriage of the mysteries and the birth of *the* divine child. Paradoxically it is the failure of this attempt to play the goddess and use her powers on the human child that recalls her to her true goddess nature. She remembers who she is, reveals herself, and im-mediately begins to prepare for the passing on of her vision, her essence, on an altogether different level—the symbolic level of the mysteries.

Demeter's center of gravity has changed, and she orders a temple to be built for her in Eleusis. It seems totally illogical that at *this* point she orders the temple to be built, for there is still a long road to be traveled before the opposites can be reconciled, before that which is to be worshiped and experienced at Eleusis is understood by Demeter herself. But myth, particularly feminine myth, is not logical. Its truth is of another order. Demeter has emerged from her wholly personal grief; she consciously knows that she is living a great mystery and that, no matter how long her suffering may last, the end of it is certain. The *hierosgamos*, the holy marriage, which is the unity of all opposites, is an established possibility—she *remembers* her true nature. It is a moment of recognition, a kind of remembering of that which somewhere at bottom we have always known. The current problems are not solved, the conflicts remain, but such a person's suffering, as long as he or she does not evade it, will no longer lead to neurosis but to new life. The individual intuitively glimpses who he is.

So the goddess remembers herself and builds her temple, within which she now encloses herself, and in which she sits down again in a grief more terrible than before. It is not regression; it is her cave of introversion. Whereas at first she had simply surrendered to her sorrow, she now enters consciously into it. She is in a ritual, holy place, contained. She does not yet know the solution, but she herself must accept the dark, and inner death, if her daughter is ever to return to the light of day. And as the goddess withdrew, so the earth dried up and withered, the sap of growth departed, and the land lay dying. The wasteland around the Fisher King in the Grail legend carries the same meaning— when it is time for a transformation of the whole personality, the birth of a totally new attitude, everything dries up inwardly and outwardly and life becomes more and more sterile until the *conscious* mind is forced to recognize the gravity of the situation, is compelled to accept the validity of the unconscious.

The gods now become frantic at what is happening on earth—pretty soon there will be no more men to worship the mighty gods of reason! As always happens, they get busy *bribing* Demeter to emerge from her temple and her sorrow—urging her to settle for a pleasant life of peace and honor on Olympus and to forget about her daughter down below, who can be left to keep the dark powers happy and prevent them from bothering the upper gods. So does reason and the fear of the dark speak to us.

"Even if my greatest value does stay buried forever, it is foolish and arrogant of me to make so much fuss about it. I must conquer my misery, stop thinking about it, make the best of things as they are. Surely the great god Zeus must know best, and he is offering me ease and a position of great importance." But Demeter does not for a moment yield to good-sense arguments. There can be no halfway solution, no stopping at the state of separation of the opposites. She is deaf to all the entreaties and appeals of every god in turn. She uses the invincible weapon of the woman who, when something utterly irrational and against all conscious values rises up from the root of her being, simply sits still and refuses to budge. No man can resist this, but unfortunately we too often use this tool when we are moved not by a real intuition from our roots but by our overpowering emotional possessiveness or an animus opinion.

The gods give in to Demeter, of course, and at last the conscious and the unconscious, the masculine and the feminine, begin to pull together. It seems at first simply a capitulation of consciousness to the regressive longing of the mother. Zeus sends Hermes to tell Hades he must give Persephone back and restore the status quo, for Zeus himself cannot produce the solution which reconciles the opposites. Only when Hades, the Lord of Death, Zeus's dark brother, will cooperate can the answer come. It is he who gives Persephone the seed of the pomegranate to eat —and she, who has hitherto rejected all food (refused to assimilate the experience), now in the moment when she is full of joy at the thought of not having to accept it, takes the pomegranate seed involuntarily, but voluntarily swallows it. In spite of her protests, she really has no intention of regressing to identification with her mother again. This is an image of how the saving thing can happen in the unconscious before the conscious mind can grasp at all what is going on. There are many dreams in which the dreamer tries to return to an old thing or situation but finds, for example, the doors barred or the telephone broken. The ego still yearns for the status quo, but further down the price has been paid, and we *can't* go back. Hence the great value of dreams in making us aware of these movements below. Even Demeter, in her conscious planning, still half yearns for her daughter to return as before; but her questioning is quite perfunctory. As soon as she knows the seed has been eaten, there is no more said on the subject—all is joy. Persephone has eaten the food of Hades, has taken the seed of the dark into herself and can now give birth to her own new personality. So also can her mother. They have both passed through death to the renewal of a new spring—the inward renewal which age need never lose—and have accepted the equal necessity of winter and life in the darkness of the underworld.

The two become Demeter-Kore instead of Demeter and Kore. Now, to complete the unity, Hecate joins the others; she too is united to Persephone, becoming from that day her "queenly comrade," mother, maiden, and sibyl—the threefold nature of woman made whole. The images unite; they no longer merge or fight or possess each other, and the woman who knows this experience becomes "one in herself."

THE MYSTERIES

Demeter, united to her daughter, taught the rulers of Eleusis her rites and her mysteries, and these mysteries were for a thousand years a center of the inner religious life of antiquity. It is a measure of the power and depth of experience of the initiates that in all this time the secrets were never revealed by any one of the vast numbers involved. The merest hints leaked out, so that we can only know that certain symbols played a part, but very little about the rituals which led to the final revelation.

It is certain that the rites were not a mystery-drama, not an acting out of the story of the two goddesses, though each element of the myth was *symbolically* experienced. The initiates gathered in Athens on the first day—anyone could be a candidate if he spoke Greek and was not guilty of the shedding of blood—and went through a purification ritual of bathing in the sea. Probably they had already been through the lesser mysteries of Persephone at Agrai in which water and darkness played a major part, and the candidate experienced the passive suffering of the raped Persephone in the underworld through a conscious act of surrender. After the bathing there was a procession to Eleusis of the purified, bearing torches. Various symbolic actions were performed along the way, and on arrival outside Eleusis there was a time of fasting. The journey and the fasting were the symbols of Demeter's nine days of wandering and grief; Eleusis itself was the place of the *finding*.

It is probable that the rites proper began with a dance. Euripides wrote that on the night of the dance around the "fountain in the square of beautiful dances—the stormy heaven of Zeus begins to dance also, the moon and the fifty daughters of Nereus, the goddesses of the sea and the ever flowing rivers, all dance in honor of the golden-crowned maiden and her holy mother." Already the individual is lifted out of his small, rational, personal ego, and the whole universe is dancing with him.

There was also, it is thought, a communion drink—meal and water, probably, as drunk by Demeter in the king's hall, and the rites moved on through we know not what pattern to the climax of a ritual marriage by violence—not, as one might expect, that of Hades with Persephone, but the marriage of Demeter and Zeus. These are the mysteries of Demeter (not of Persephone, except insofar as she is an aspect of Demeter), of the Great Mother, whose experience of loss and finding led her to the *hieros-gamos*, the union of the earth with the creator god, which means the birth of the divine child who is the "whole."

After the sacred marriage, a great light shone and the cry of the hierophant range out: "The great goddess has borne a sacred child— Brimo has borne Brimos." The goddess has acquired a new name which means "the strong one," "the power to arouse terror." Without terror, without experience of the terrible face of God, there can be no divine birth. It must be remembered that Persephone also, in her dark, negative aspect, is Medusa, the Gorgon's head, which she herself sends forth from the underworld—"a monstrosity," says Kerenyi, "the nocturnal aspect of what by day is the most desirable of all things." The birth of the child who bears the name Brimo alone can resolve the intolerable tension of these opposites, the child who is Demeter, Persephone, Hecate, Zeus, and Hades in one living image. The child is a boy, but also a girl, the androgynous fruit of the holy marriage. It is known that a single child initiate played a part in the mysteries, and that this could be either a boy or a girl, as the omens should decide.

The marriage and the birth, however, were not the final revelation. The most profound vision of all, the actual experience of immortality, came in deep silence, when a mown ear of grain was held up and *seen* by the initiate. Nor can words ever accompany such an experience. The ancients said that at this point the idea of immortality "lost everything confusing and became a satisfying vision."

The mown ear of grain is a perfect symbol of immortality, of eternal rebirth. It is the fruit of life, the harvest, which feeds and nourishes, it is the seed which must sink into the earth and disappear in order to give birth again. It is mown down in the moment of its ripeness, as Persephone was mown down and torn from her mother, as every achievement in our lives outer or inner must be mown down in order to give birth to the new. It is the mother who nourishes, it is the seed of the father, and it is the child born of them both, in one image. The elevated Host in the Mass is the same symbol, the same silent epiphany, "showing forth" of immortality, with a tremendous added dimension. Bread is that which has been produced by man from the raw grain. *Consciousness* is added to the purely natural symbol, for Christ has consciously lived the myth. His initiates too must experience the mowing down, the burial and the rising again in a conscious realization of the Christ within. "Unless a corn of wheat fall into the ground and die, it remaineth alone, but if it die, it bringeth forth much fruit." That which must die is not the evil and the ugly but the thing of greatest beauty and meaning, the maiden of stainless innocence, so that we may finally know that over which death has no power.

There is evidence that the final act at Eleusis was the setting up of two vessels which were tipped over, so that the water flowed toward the east and the west, the directions of birth and death. Thus the ritual began and ended with water, symbol of the unconscious beginnings of all life and of the wise spirit of the conscious end—the living water "springing up into eternal life."

It should be stressed that the rites at Eleusis were neither an allegory nor a miracle but a mystery. An allegory exists in the realm of ordinary knowledge; it is a metaphor, a story, reflecting, for example, the cycle of the seasons or speaking of the living on of man in his descendants—facts which we all know of but which have for the most part little power to affect or change our personalities. As Kerenyi says, "There is a vast difference between knowing *of* something and knowing it and being it." Of the difference between miracle and mystery, he writes that a miracle causes people to talk endlessly about it, whereas the true mysteries are kept silent so that they may transform us from within through the symbols which in Jung's words "alone can reconcile the warring opposites, conveying to man in a single image that which is thought *and* feeling and beyond them both."

The Homeric hymn ends with the words "awful mysteries which no one may in any way transgress or pry into or utter, for deep awe of the gods checks the voice. Happy is he among men upon earth who has seen these mysteries; but he who is uninitiated and who has no part in them never has lot of like good things once he is dead, down in the darkness and gloom." The ancient hymn thus asserts the three essentials of all the mystery rituals of all the religions. First, the rites must not be transgressed, altered in any way; second, they must be accepted without analysis and without question; third, they must not be spoken of, must be kept absolutely secret.

It is immediately obvious that modern man, even in the Roman Church which has been the guardian of the Christian mysteries for so long, is busy breaking all these essentials of a ritual mystery. We are changing it, we pry into everything, and we speak about it all incessantly. The element of awe is being deliberately banished. All this is not something which can or should be avoided. The growth of consciousness inevitably and rightly means that we pry into, we question everything with our hungry minds, and to try to stop this would be futile obscurantism. But it is equally futile and an arrogant folly to imagine that, having banished the mystery from our outer cults, we can now dispense with it altogether. Then indeed we shall end up in the "darkness and gloom," denying reality to the psyche itself and its truths. Without vision, without mystery, all of our fine intellectual understanding and its great values turn to dust.

The hymn refers to the fate of the initiate after death. In this context Kerenyi writes, "The 'eidola' in the realm of the dead . . . are the images with which the deceased individual, through his uniqueness, has enriched the world." Only to the extent that a man has lived his unique individual meaning does he attain to immortality. Persephone was called "the eternally unique" because she had united the two worlds, the dark and the light.

Surely the meaning of the dogma *extra ecclesiam nulla salus* is that there is no salvation without experience of the mystery. It became a cruel and bigoted statement when it was interpreted in the literal outer sense (a kind of interpretation from which all the great dogmas of the Church have suffered immeasurably), and it gave sanction to such horrors as the Inquisition. The ecumenical movement today is tackling this distortion on its own level with arguments of reason and good sense, but it misses the essential point, which is that man should recognize and experience the level of his being where this dogma is eternally and *individually* true. Outside the "Church," outside the mystery, there is no salvation.

When the outer cult loses its "mana" for a man, then the mystery falls into the unconscious and must there be rediscovered by the individual journeying alone in the dark places to the experience of the symbols within. When images of power and beauty rise up in dreams or fantasies, they make an immediate impact. We are in awe before them. Sometimes there comes a specific dream of initiation which may alter the whole course of a man's life. Such images are not something thought up or pried into, they cannot be altered, and instinctively we sense that they must not be spoken of except to another "initiate." When one does expose them wrongly, one can *feel* the power go out of them. Although their details are individual, unique, they link a man to the whole experience of mankind, and their impact can be immensely increased through a knowledge of the content and meaning of ancient myth, of the eternal themes which have embodied through the ages the truths of the human psyche. Our individual images may invoke, perhaps, the dance of the primitive, or the flood, or Demeter-Kore, Isis-Osiris, the Buddha's Flower sermon, the Zen master's koan, and, for us in the West most powerfully of all, the birth and death of Christ, the bread and wine of the Mass. The analyzing mind which has destroyed mystery is thus linked again to the immediacy of the inner experience, and the redeeming symbol is reborn.

STRAW AND GOLD:
CONSCIOUSNESS
AND THE
MATURE WOMAN

Most people have heard of Rumpelstiltskin and have a vague idea that the story is concerned with the finding of a name, a theme so fascinating to humankind that it makes some impression even on the uninterested. There are many versions of the story but they differ only in details. It tells of a peasant girl whose father is continually boasting of her merits, even asserting that she has the power to spin straw into gold. The king hears of this and sends his servants to fetch the girl, demanding that she spin some straw for him. When no gold appears, he shuts her up for a night, saying that, if the straw becomes gold by morning, he will make her queen, but, if not, she will have her head cut off. She is in despair, her task being a human impossibility. Yet she is one of those who still know in their hearts that the impossible can happen, and so there appears a little man who, when he hears her dilemma, rocks with merry laughter, since to him the job presents no problem at all. He will spin the straw into gold for her, but he exacts a price. When she becomes queen, she must give him her first child. The girl accepts. She marries the king and has a child, and all is happiness until the little man comes to claim the child. Then indeed she weeps and implores him for mercy, until finally he consents to let her off on one condition. She must find out what his name is. She guesses and guesses—every name she can think of or imagine. She sends servants far and wide to seek strange names, but all in vain. She is at the end of all hope when at the last moment a friend comes who has been walking in the forest and heard the little man singing to himself that his name is Rumpelstiltskin. So when he comes to the queen for his final answer, she tells his name, and he is so furious that he grabs his foot and tears himself to pieces.

Fairy stories almost always have this character of "all or nothing"— reflecting a basic truth of the psyche. Tolerance is a major virtue but, like all virtues, it may be displaced from its proper level. It then turns into a soft, corrupting attitude blinding us to the basic "either-or" at the roots of life. In the imagery of the story, either we must turn the straw of our lives into gold, in which case we will marry the king, that is, find the royal creative meaning of our lives and bring forth our "child"; or, if we fail to do so, we will lose our heads, lose all possibility of coming to individual consciousness.

We should first think for a moment about the father's role in getting his daughter into this pickle. We are all very ready to go back and lay the blame for our troubles on our parents' blindness—and to recognize their mistakes is usually an essential step along the way. But, as we look deeper, we see that it is precisely to these mistakes that we owe the stimulus which forces us to seek the truth in our own way, if we will pay the price. The girl's father does a terrible thing to her because of his selfish pride. His guilt remains, but for her it is, we may imagine, the only thing which could have forced her to face the basic "either-or" and so launched her on her own unique and "royal" way.

How do we spin the straw of our lives into gold? Fundamentally it is a matter of a glimpse, a momentary, intuitive glimpse at this stage, of the ultimate truth beyond the opposites, that straw and gold are one thing. Who is the little man, coming from the unconscious where the opposites are one, without whom we cannot break through to this glimpse? For him the task is easy. He is a dwarf figure from under the earth, passionate and violent, wise and cunning, angry and merry, a creature of extremes, of childish affects, and to the young (or to the young part of us) he brings that breakthrough of passion, or romantic love, which turns the world to gold and makes the impossible possible. A boy or girl, if he or she is to plunge into life in any real way, *must* fall in love with someone or something. This does not refer of course to the easy, promiscuous, so-called "falling in love" which is mere appetite, but to the true romantic love, of which Charles Williams has so beautifully written. This love is a glimpse of the ultimate glory, which cannot last in that form but is nonetheless valid and beautiful. "Unless devotion is given to the thing which must prove false in the end, the thing that is true in the end cannot enter." Devotion is the key word. The little man is that which releases in us a passionate devotion—to a person, to an idea, to an art—awakening in us that vivid perception of beauty in one thing which can transfigure the whole of our world to gold. Thus the little man brings that moment in a man's or woman's life when he or she is committed without reservation to a love, a vision, a task, entering into life without thought of risk and accepting the basic "either-or." So one finds that the dirtiest bit of straw can turn to pure gold, and one is launched on the way that can lead over the years to maturity and the possibility of wholeness.

This little man, however, who comes to our help from the unconscious, is, as always with unconscious contents, an ambiguous figure. He is both friend and enemy, and, like Lucifer, he is both the bringer of light (*lucem ferre* means to carry light) and the threat of disaster. He brings to the girl the saving miracle, but he also exacts a price. The miracle will carry her to great happiness and success, but she must give up her child when he is born. So she makes a thoughtless promise, but it is also unconscious acceptance of future struggle. In accepting passion and the great release of energy it brings, we accept the resulting danger, and the price that is exacted is perhaps the one thing that prevents us from getting stuck in our infantile identification with our achievements. The romantic projection, so essential to youth, is extremely destructive in maturity, and so at the moment of the birth of the new, most precious value comes the little man again, shaking us awake by threatening the child. "I saved you before; now give the child to me." This is most plainly seen outwardly in the contrast between the "romantic" possessive mother, emotionally identified with her child, and the creative mother, who nourishes her child and sets him free. The latter has found the little man's name.

We can watch this pattern not only in the span of a lifetime but in the frequent ups and downs of the inner life. We experience a breakthrough of consciousness, the birth of a new potentiality demanding a new kind of commitment, and immediately we are tempted to romanticize this new vision, to possess and identify with it, which means that it will pass into the power of that ambiguous, emotionally unstable little man and sink again into the unconscious. Only on one condition can the child be saved, and paradoxically it is the threatener himself who offers the chance of salvation. We must consciously be able to *name* this elusive power within us.

There was once a British Broadcasting Company program called "Kafka, Rilke, and Rumpelstiltskin," in which Idris Parry defined Rumpelstiltskin in his unnamed state as "a confusion of boundless possibilities." Our way to maturity could be defined as a long and arduous effort to name these possibilities, to name our reactions and our complexes, so that, instead of alternately being carried by them or drowned in them, we may find them a source of controlled strength. With the name there comes to us the power of detachment and of conscious choice.

The power of the *Name* is a great and holy theme in all religion and myth, in the whole history of consciousness. The name is the word, the symbol of that which separates man from the beast, from unconscious nature, and with it comes power. Adam named the beasts, and with the naming came his domination over them. Primitives are extremely careful about the speaking of names. If an enemy knows a man's name, he automatically gains power over him. Even today the signing of a man's name is an irrevocable commitment, a handing over of power to someone else.

In the name of God resides his power. At baptism, which is the ritual of entering into potential conscious union with the divine, a child is given his or her unique personal name, "In the Name of the Father, the Son, and the Holy Ghost." Man has through the ages believed that by speaking the name of God in purity of motive we invoke the light-giving power of the Spirit, and that in blaspheming it we set loose the destructive power of darkness. The fact that these beliefs have lost their power in our culture in no way lessens their deep meaning in the psyche.

There are "levels" of names. A person sometimes dreams at a moment of great increase of consciousness that he has been given a new name. T. S. Eliot has written, humorously but nonetheless profoundly, of these "levels" in his poem "The Naming of Cats." The cat must have an everyday name in common use, a special name which is hers alone, and finally a secret name.

These "levels" are just as applicable to man. We have our family name, which any stranger uses; our unique, personal name only to be used by those close to us (one symptom of the lack of respect for individuality in our society is the indiscriminate use of the personal name); and finally that secret name which we seek consciously or unconsciously throughout our lives, the name which is unique and yet one, we may believe, with The Name. "To him that overcometh will I give to eat of the hidden manna, and will give him a white stone and in the stone a new name written which no man knoweth save he that receiveth it."

We know, then, that in approaching our own depths we are searching for the right names for the unseen forces within us. This is very far from arriving at a mere intellectual definition. It is the search for the true symbolic image in which we recognize the essence of the thing, a *word* in which the indefinable is expressed beyond intellectual categories. In the process of searching we bring to bear all the powers of intellect, imagination, feeling, and instinct, and then perhaps the name will become known to us as if by accident, arising spontaneously from the depths, bringing a new intuitive certainty, the Word made flesh, the union of opposites.

So it was for the girl in the story. She searched and searched, tried every name her memory or imagination could conceive, sent her servants into far countries to seek for new possibilities. For us one powerful form of this seeking can be the use of active imagination. We can talk to the figures in our dreams, inviting them to reply to us, to reveal their characters and motives. It is not easy to do this, but the effort can be immensely rewarding, as it brings together the conscious and unconscious much more dynamically than mere conscious talk *about* a dream. However, at the last, the name will break through, usually at a moment when we feel that all our efforts have been in vain, and it seems to come by chance. Not so, of course.

Idris Parry's talk is largely concerned with the nature of so-called accidents. If the finding of Rumpelstiltskin's name is a mere accident, then, he says, "the whole thing is a swindle." But coincidence truly means "the falling together of events." He quotes Kafka: "Accident is the name one gives to the coincidence of events of which one does not know the causation."

This total relevance of everything that happens is what Jung calls *synchronicity*, what Charles Williams calls *coinherence*, and what is truly meant by the *Will of God*.

Idris Parry asks what the girl had done to deserve her knowledge. The answer is "nothing." "It comes to her, she does not go to it, and she succeeds for that very reason," says Parry. Kafka says, "Stay at your table and listen. Don't even listen, just wait, be completely quiet and alone. The world will offer itself to you to be unmasked." It is not, however, entirely true that she has done nothing. She has tried with all she has to find the answer, used all her faculties in a supreme effort, and so fulfilled the essential condition for being awake enough to hear the name when it is spoken. Through this effort alone can we come to the point at which we are *able* to be still and wait in the real sense. Kafka's words express great truth, but a very dangerous one if we interpret it on the wrong level. Sitting and waiting without having made every effort of which the conscious personality is capable would be merely a matter of sloth or evasion, suspiciously like waiting to be spoonfed. Always, however, we must remember that in the end the answer will be given, not earned. The real goal of all our efforts is to arrive at the capacity for this goalless waiting. Then, indeed, the little man will sing his name, and the friend will "chance" to hear, and we shall break through to freedom and the "child" will be safe.

Why does the little man tear himself to pieces in the end? He is unbridled affect, convulsed with merry laughter, or screaming and dancing in rage. When he is named, these warring emotions in the queen are resolved in the birth of true feeling, and they tear themselves to pieces harmlessly, as their energy passes into the new consciousness of the mature woman. It is a lesser fairy-story image, perhaps, of the tearing to pieces of the god Dionysos, the dismemberment of the king in alchemy, which is the prelude to rebirth. In the fairy story the self-destruction of Rumpelstiltskin means the safety of the "child," the new possibility of wholeness in the mother. In her new mature consciousness she no longer needs to spin straw into gold, for the passionate projection of images essential to youth has yielded to the objectivity of the free individual. Straw remains straw, gold remains gold; clear and distinct in their proper function, they no longer pass one into the other but unite in the infinite pattern of the whole. This is the final miracle.

E O W Y N

In J.R.R. Tolkien's *The Lord of the Rings*, the character of Eowyn, niece-daughter of Theoden, king of the Mark, has a profound relevance to some aspects of the feminist movement in our time. In the story she is the slayer of the deadly king of the nine black Ringwraiths and her life is very different from the usual pattern of the feminine in most ancient myths and legends—for example, the way of a Penelope, whose patient waiting and indomitable love nourish the man as he goes forth to wield his sword. It will be remembered that in this twentieth-century myth no *man* could have killed the dark king, however strong or brave he might be; even Gandalf, the great wizard, was able to do no more than repulse him temporarily. Only through the woman with a sword could his power be brought to an end.

The Ringwraith's weapon was fear and despair; man and beast fled before him as panic seized them and all hope died in their hearts. On the field of Pelennor only Theoden the king, who had passed through darkness to a great awakening in his old age, stood fast when the dark king, riding on a winged beast, descended upon him. But Theoden's horse, Snowmane, terror-stricken, reared and fell upon him.

But first let us go back and trace the story of Eowyn before she took to herself the disguise of Dernhelm the young warrior, one of Theoden's knights. We first see her standing behind the throne of her uncle-father, Theoden, as he sits, old and demoralized, with Wormtongue at his feet— Wormtongue the cunning, the plausible, who has gradually undermined the old king's personality, whispering lies into his ear about his weakness and the hopelessness of any resistance to the evils of time. Wormtongue is the mouthpiece of Saruman, the corrupted wizard, who has betrayed the inner wisdom, seeking personal power and dominion. Eowyn has grown up in this atmosphere, has watched the gradual decay in the old man she loves. There is no mother, no feminine warmth, at this court, and she, as a woman, has no influence in the counsels of the king, no outlet for her generosity of spirit. She must even endure the secret knowledge that the contemptible Wormtongue is lusting after her and means to possess her at the last. She has indeed a brother, Eomer, whom she loves and trusts; he is young and brave and intelligent, but is in disgrace with the king, suspected of treason almost, through the scheming of Wormtongue.

It is very clear what this kind of situation has done to one of her nature, reared as she was on the tales of chivalry and courage of her family's past. The heroic lives only in her fantasy; in outer life she must watch betrayal and decay, and she has encased herself in armor outwardly and inwardly. No natural warmth of passion has yet touched her; the springs of her womanhood are frozen, and she longs to be a man, to fight, to conquer or to die in battle wielding a sword in place of that which Theoden has given into the keeping of Wormtongue. She has become the shield maiden of Rohan, beautiful but cold—cold as a woman, that is, but not cold—indeed consumed with frustration and passion in the regions of her burning spirit.

As we read, we must surely feel how all this mirrors the predicament of many women in this century. Born into a family in which, perhaps, the father has succumbed to the softness of his anima while the mother, as mother, is simply absent, since she is buried in a mass of animus opinions, the daughter is brought up without a clear image of either masculine or feminine, while all around her the decay in the collective attitudes dominating consciousness presses in upon her. The betrayals of Saruman and the whisperings of Wormtongue have achieved unprecedented power in our society. The old virtues of honor and justice and the values of eros, of individual relatedness, are in grave danger. The Nazgul (human beings who had given their whole lives to serving the Dark Lord and who have become like wraiths) are indeed abroad in the land, mounted not as before, on ordinary horses (instinct still in normal form though turned to dark purposes), but on the monstrously evil and archaic winged beasts. This horror may be recognized, perhaps, in the utter sense-lessness of so much violence and lust in our society and in the spread of the present terrorist attitude to life in the abuse of children.

What has been the effect of all this on women of great potential warmth and nobility? Like Eowyn, they grow up either determined to enter the battle on the masculine level, fighting with all they have for a cause or an idea, or, at the opposite pole, succumb to the lust of Wormtongue and an indiscriminate instinctual sexuality which, cut off from relationship, ends by destroying eros itself. Nevertheless there are not a few who come, as did Eowyn, through suffering and courage, to find their wholeness as women.

We may indeed hope that the shocks of recent years will be to our time like the shock of Gandalf's staff breaking the spell over Theoden, restoring to him his sword, sending him forth on his last great ride to his death and the rising of a new king, a new conscious ruler. If so, then indeed, as in the War of the Ring—the war which was to substitute love and the value of the individual for the ruling demon of power—the moment is upon us when victory will hang upon the readiness of women to confront the most powerful of all the dark forces ranged against us— that which no man can conquer with his sword, that which is vulnerable only to the newly found sword of the feminine spirit.

The Nazgul king is the image of the despair which can undermine even the best and the bravest among us; it is a despair born of the emptiness, the isolation and lack of communication and consequent loss of meaning which is overwhelming our culture. It is a bisexual image: the mind of man turned demonic in its intellectual pride, emptied of human compassion, rides in the air on the mindless beast into which the instinc-tive feminine regresses when human beings reject the values of the heart. The inevitable outcome of this unholy union is the despair which breeds first indifference and ultimately active cruelty and violence in all its forms.

Let us watch the phases of Eowyn's journey. In the moment of Theoden's awakening, she has looked upon Aragorn, the carrier of the new consciousness of the Self, the king of the future. For the first time she experiences romantic love; but, like so many women of her type who have grown afraid of their femininity and are shut off from it, she projects her animus onto a man whom she unconsciously knows to be unattainable. He carries for her her inner image of a heroic figure who personifies her fantasies of great deeds, who compensates for the pitiful failure of the father. Her love for Theoden has been deeply wounded—has gradually turned to pity and unconscious contempt. In Aragorn she sees her ideals in human form, but, as he so clearly perceives, she remains cold; she does not see him as a person. She longs to join him not as a woman but as a companion warrior on his quest—to follow him in *his* way, not hers. He refuses her with great compassion as he rides away on the Paths of the Dead, and she is left with a frozen heart but a fierce determination not to be left behind when Theoden rides to war.

Theoden also refuses her his permission to go with the Riders. He refuses without understanding, with the usual hackneyed masculine lecture on woman's place being in the home. But Eowyn, like all awakened women since this century began, knows that, if she accepts this platitude any longer and refuses to stand by her certainty that she has the courage and the ability to "wield a sword," then her creative spirit will wither and die, and despair will finally destroy her. It is absolutely essential for Eowyn at this point that she defy the father's authority—as it became essential for modern woman to rebel and to disobey and to enter the arena of the male-dominated world. And at first, like Eowyn, in order to free themselves, they have been compelled to disguise themselves as men —and many have come to imagine that there really is no difference anymore. They forget they are disguised and so identify with the emerging spirit.

It is, however, precisely at this point in the story that Eowyn's repressed and despised femininity begins to assert itself from her unconscious. It is the crucial moment for every woman who is driven by the creative spirit into the Logos world. Will she imitate man, in which case her spirit will turn sterile and demonic; or will she, in the midst of her intoxicating freedom, be true to her basic nature? If she chooses the latter, then indeed she may come at infinite cost to confront and destroy that fell wraith, riding on the beast of cruelty and greed, who yields to no power but that of the true woman who has dared to grasp the sword of the spirit.

We see then Eowyn, disguised as Dernhelm, young and slender, sitting on her horse, whose name is Windfola, as the men of Rohan gather and prepare to set forth on their great ride to the battle with the Dark Lord. Sitting there, she hears Theoden saying farewell to Merry, the hobbit, and forbidding him to go with them. "You are too small, though stout of heart. You could do nothing but get in the way. You must stay here with the women and children." She sees in despair the misery, so like her own, in Merry's eyes, and as the companies depart she rides up to him and offers to take him up behind her on her horse, which can easily carry them both.

It would be hard indeed to conceive of any young man, going forth to his first battle to prove his courage and his manhood, who would consider for a moment such a thing. Yet Eowyn, intoxicated as she must have been by the coming fulfillment of her daydreams, suddenly sees Merry as a person and is filled with compassion. It is a truly feminine reaction. No matter how it may restrict and encumber her new freedom, she cannot leave him behind. She is only *disguised* as a man. Symbolically seen, she takes with her on her journey the childlike earth-wisdom in the person of the small hobbit. We are reminded of the Kabiri, the little earth men who accompany the goddesses of the ancient world. Her heroic fantasy world is suddenly "earthed," we may say, by the strong infusion of "hobbit sense."

As the host of Rohan sweep into battle, Merry notices that Dernhelm keeps as close as he can to the king. All fly before the sword of Theoden, but be it noted that Eowyn has not yet drawn her sword, though all fight around her. She does not in fact draw it until she hears the voice of the Nazgul as she stands over the body of her uncle-father to protect it from the foul beast. She had spoken of fighting like a man with men, but in the heat of the battle the inherent strength of her womanhood instinctively takes over. She cannot kill for any cause, however great, simply to conquer. She can only kill to save a person whom she loves.

The woman's way of redemption through all the ages is the giving of her life's blood for another. But it is no longer so simple for the Eowyn of our time. She is equally willing to die for another, but first she must draw the sword of her spirit—the sword of her conscious discrimination, of her intelligence and her imagination. With this sword she destroys first the devouring monster of greed and then with all her feminine strength she strikes into the head (he has no heart) of that ghostlike horror of the masculine spirit turned demonic, which would destroy not only her personally but also all warmth of human kindness and therefore all hope in our civilization.

We may learn much from the few lines describing Eowyn as she struck this blow. First, when the winged beast plunged its claws into the body of Snowmane, her father's horse, and was about to devour both dead horse and king, she raised her voice in defiance. "Begone foul dwimmerlaik, lord of carrion! Leave the dead in peace!" A major cause of our despair lies surely in the fact that, as traditional moral codes and rigid standards of behavior inevitably and rightly crumble and die, men have fallen disastrously into contempt for the human and divine values on which those codes, however outdated in form, were originally based. The heroic figure of King Theoden on his white horse of chivalry must indeed die, but if his body were to be torn to pieces and devoured by the shadow king and his beast, no transformation of his heroism could take place. Instead of a new birth of the dead hero on a deeper level of awareness, which alone can save us in the era which is dawning, the old attitudes are simply replaced, eaten up, by empty despair.

One of the basic qualities of the feminine psyche is its capacity for total devotion. A mother in defense of her child will stop at nothing; a woman's love once truly given to a person is the most tenacious thing in nature, and no collective or moral standards of any kind have power to alter this devotion. A mature woman whose love is purged of possessiveness will risk everything to save a person—any person—from destruction. (The negative side of this is, of course, a woman possessed by a shadow-animus combination who gives *blind* devotion to a cause or a person.) Eowyn on the field of Pelennor is an archetypal picture of a modern woman who can no longer, as in past centuries, simply offer passively to give her blood. How the Nazgul would laugh! No, she must actively use her sword, but in that moment she has no thought of causes or of her own wish to be as like a man as possible. The hand which wields the sword of her spirit is wholly a woman's hand. Faced with the threat of the worst that despair can do to mind and body, she laughs in face of the horror. "Do what you will—but I will hinder it, if I may." She will defend the integrity of personal devotion, of the human heart, to the death and beyond. And now she reveals herself with pride and joy as a woman indeed. "Thou fool. No living man may hinder me," he cries, and she answers:

"But no living man am I! You look upon a woman. Eowyn I am, Eomund's daughter. You stand between me and my lord and kin. Begone, if you be not deathless! For living or dark undead, I will smite you, if you touch him."

Tolkien further tells us: "Her eyes grey as the sea were hard and fell, and yet tears were on her cheek."

So many women have forgotten how to weep that they have lost the meaning of tears. "Women must weep": this is not a badge of weakness; it is an essential strength. (Weak tears of self-pity are of course quite another thing.) Eowyn's cheeks are wet at the moment of her greatest masculine act.

The king of despair now raised his great black mace to destroy Eowyn. It is worth noting that the Nazgul does not fight with a discriminating sword, but with an annihilating club. He shattered her frail shield and broke her arm, but Merry, the small earthbound hobbit, whose strength had been rejected by the heroic Theoden but recognized by Eowyn, saw with love and wonder the slender woman standing there in her beauty and courage, her sword gleaming in her hand, and he rose from his own groveling terror to help her in her need. Plunging his own sword into the Nazgul's leg, he enabled the woman with her last strength to drive her sword into the head under the crown, and the king of despair in that age of the world dissolved into nothingness before Merry's eyes, while Eowyn herself lay as one dead. It was then that the old king regained consciousness for a moment. He saw only Merry, and he passed away in peace and honor instead of in horror, speaking gently words of good hope for those who would create a new world after him, for Eomer and Eowyn whom he loved but could not understand. The old era would be transformed, not destroyed.

At exactly the same time that this meeting took place between the woman and the king of the Nazgul, another battle with the great enemy, despair, was going on in the citadel of Gondor. The steward of Gondor, Denethor, long threatened by this enemy, became completely and crazily possessed by it when he heard of the fear of the Nazgul that was running through the city, and he carried his wounded son Faramir into the burial places of the kings and there tried to set fire to himself and his son. Faramir was saved by Gandalf, the wise man, but Gandalf would have arrived too late had it not been for two simple people. First, once again, a hobbit was the essential link, and, secondly, there was the simple soldier, Beregond, who with great moral courage retained his sense of *personal* values in the midst of disintegration.

The synchronicity of this with the victory of Eowyn and Merry is obvious; and almost immediately afterward comes the final victory in this battle, with the arrival of Aragorn, sailing up the river after his ordeal on the Paths of the Dead. Without any one of these men of integrity and true feeling, there could have been no going on to the final defeat of the Dark Lord, and the destruction of the Ring of Power by Frodo could not have succeeded. It is, however, abundantly clear that, after the sword of Eowyn had brought about the dissolution of the Nazgul king, the armies of Gondor were freed from the terrible contagion of despair which would have frustrated all the attempts of Gandalf and Aragorn to lead them to the last battle at the gates of Mordor. No man in that last battle had any illusion about the likelihood, the almost certainty, of defeat and death; but that is a very different thing from despair. Indeed the capacity to face defeat and death is the proof of the victory of faith over despair, as Winston Churchill wrote.

This, then, I believe, is the great challenge to modern woman. Unless she can find the courage and the vision, the individual freedom of spirit, to plunge her sword into the head of the despair which threatens human-ity, then hope wanes and darkness thickens upon us. It is no longer enough for woman to act instinctively as a link to the wisdom in the unconscious for man. We have drifted so far away from this wisdom into sterility that an instinctive return means the all too familiar fall into violence and sensuality. What an image it is—the black terror of the Ringwraith riding an obscenely horrible beast! Therefore the woman must not simply "know" the spirit (instinctively and unconsciously as in the past), but—to quote Charles Williams's telling phrase—must "know she knows," and so she consciously takes up the sword to slay both beast and wraith so that the shadow may pass and man may remember in his heart as well as his head the undying spark over which defeat and death have no power. And she must do this as woman, not at all in imitation of man. If she falls into this imitation, then her sword thrusts become mere pinpricks which succeed only in wounding the masculinity of the men around her.

In an individual's life, what does this mean? It means that, brought up in a world of dominant masculinity, she must work throughout her life, in small things as in great, to discriminate her feelings, her eros values, from all the conventional opinions and secondhand convictions which beset her animus and freeze her womanhood, and at the same time she must affirm the great gulf which lies between eros and the possessive concupiscence into which her instinctual emotions can so easily drive her. She will need great courage if she is to recognize and confront the half-conscious plotting and scheming of the animus in order to get her own way, prove herself in the right. Thus she enters on the quest for her true identity as an individual woman. The way will bring her into dark-ness and loneliness, through fire and water, but at the last she will begin to discover consciously that unpossessive love between persons which brings renewal of faith in life itself and finally the *agape* of wholeness. The modern woman, deeply threatened as she is by the power of present-day collective unconscious forces, cannot possibly achieve this mission unless she wields the sword of the *imaginative* spirit as Eowyn did. We must never forget that, in the words of Rollo May, "Imagination is the life-blood of Eros," and that without imagination in its true sense there is no creative spirit, and no harmony between instinct and intellect is possible.

Robert Grinnell, in his book, *Alchemy of a Modern Woman*, says that a woman of today who has lost contact with her feminine nature will find herself

> *in the situation of trying to be a hero-animus, and so, having blocked Eros and the approaches to her feeling, she is over-shadowed by the monster, the archaic feminine. . . . But it is the hero-animus who must lead her forth from a mythological destiny into life and awaken awareness of her anima nature. Only so can she become a leader of man's soul.*

In another place Grinnell writes that a modern woman's "transformational activity has a certain bisexual quality which is mercurial rather than strictly feminine. She performs heroic tasks. But these have something of the character of ancient ceremonies and rituals rather than raiding expeditions."

These passages beautifully illuminate the meaning of Eowyn's story. Her hero-animus had blocked her feeling as long as she identified with him. But, standing on the field of battle, she declares herself a woman with tears of love for Theoden in her eyes and, wielding the sword of the animus power within her, she performs her heroic task. It does indeed have the quality of a ritual, transforming act and is far removed from the imagery of the conquering hero.

Eowyn was carried into Gondor and lay near death. But then came Aragorn, whose image she had truly loved with all the idealistic generosity of her heart. Aragorn is the king, and the true king, symbol of the Self as known to men, has healing hands; and he calls her back from the borders of despair and death; for in confronting the evil thing one is inevitably infected by it. Her devotion to the royal image within her, to the highest and noblest attitude she knew, now draws her back into life. Eowyn does not yet know the change that has been wrought in her, as so often we do not know at first. She still believes, as she slowly regains strength, that there is no meaning in life for her but to seek death in battle like a man. But when so deep an inner change has taken place, there comes always the event from outside which brings the new birth into consciousness.

Faramir, too, is recovering from his wound and his terrifying experience. He and Eowyn are left behind in Gondor and must wait, inactive, while the last battle is fought. And now in the shadow of their near certainty of the end of all they have loved in the world, Eowyn discovers at last that she is fully and completely a woman. Love awakens in her— not for a hero figure but for a flesh-and-blood man on this earth. The ice around her heart is melted, and in their whole and conscious commitment to each other we recognize in Faramir and Eowyn a man whose heart is alive with feminine sensitivity and a woman whose masculine courage and intelligence have been tried in the fire. They are equals in every true sense of the word, but Faramir is a man; Eowyn is a woman— there is no mixing. They are an image of the marriage of Heaven and Earth, within themselves and with each other.

No effort of all the men of good will, essential as it is, would have sufficed to save the world without the spirit of Eowyn, the woman; and if the shield maiden of Rohan had not passed through those long years during which the sword of her spirit was forged while her natural femininity lay submerged, the vital blow at the root of despair could not have been struck.

ORUAL

In his novel *Till We Have Faces*, C. S. Lewis has reexamined the ancient myth of Eros and Psyche, incorporating into it the character of Orual, a woman whose nature and character we cannot fail to recognize as contemporary. Her story concerns a woman's long search for her true face, for her identity as a person. Like most of us, she runs from this discovery for the greater part of her life: she lives behind a veil, and she refuses to hear the innermost voice of her soul. Only when she comes to that moment when she stands in a dream before the divine judge does she hear the hidden words by which she has evaded reality and the meaning of love for so long, and only then can she finally know her own face:

> *The complaint [against the gods] was the answer. To have heard myself making it was to be answered. Lightly men talk of saying what they mean. . . . When the time comes to you at which you will be forced at last to utter the speech which has lain at the center of your soul for years, which you have, all that time, idiot-like, been saying over and over, you'll not talk about joy of words. I saw well why the gods do not speak to us openly, nor let us answer. Till that word can be dug out of us, why should they hear the babble that we think we mean? How can they meet us face to face till we have faces?*

The first part of the book consists of Orual's lifelong complaint against the gods. She is, as it were, a female Job, and she dares what we must all dare if we are to know the reality of God. The second part of the story, written just before her death, is only about fifty pages long compared with the two hundred and fifty of the first part. In it the facts of her life, told with such searching honesty in the first part, unite with the myth and are filled with conscious meaning. So it is that, seeing her innermost self at last, she stands face to face with Eros, with Love itself.

At the beginning of this second part Orual says:

> What began the change was the very writing itself. Let no one lightly set about such a work. . . . The change which the writing wrought in me . . . was only a beginning—only to prepare me for the gods' surgery. They used my own pen to probe my wound.

A modern woman in this world of alienation from eros must take up this work or succumb to possession by the animus; and she must take it up with the same kind of honesty that Orual achieved, and which is of all things the most difficult for a woman caught by the inferior masculine spirit in her unconscious life.

This work is not necessarily the actual writing of one's life story in a literal sense; that may or may not be a part of it. But there must be a creative battle with "the word" in some form or other, for the word is the power of conscious definition and discrimination, while at the same time all language is symbolic. Nothing kills the symbolic life so quickly as words reduced to mere information or mindless chatter. There can be no awareness of the uniting myth without this battle to discriminate and to separate, but if women leave this work to the animus disconnected from their womanhood, then they never glimpse their true story. In the Christian myth, the Word, the Logos, must become flesh if man is to stand face to face with God, and this, a fact so consistently forgotten, is an impossibility unless he is conceived and brought to birth by woman.

The ancient way of unconscious mediation by woman of the inner wisdom is no longer enough for us today. The word in modern woman must become flesh within her own psyche by conscious creative work through her imagination, undertaken in *partnership* with the animus who relates her to her hitherto unconscious powers of discrimination. The form of this work no one can dictate. It must be discovered by the individual herself, and it may be something very simple. It is not necessarily a matter of becoming a notable artist or writer, but nevertheless, it is a task demanding immense courage and perseverance in the teeth of weakness, failure, and even despair until, as in Orual, the surgery is finished. Then indeed will come the "death before death" of which the god spoke to Orual. Myth and fact will then be known as one; her sister Psyche, whose name tells us her meaning, will be transformed and the god revealed.

In the long journey of Orual from childhood to old age we can see the terrible blows that wounded her feminine nature, her attempt to deny the numinous, her retreat into the masculine, her fight with the gods—and through it all the integrity and courage that brought her to her final beauty and wholeness.

Orual was the elder of two daughters of the king of Glome; the story begins, symbolically enough, with the death of her mother. The small kingdom of Glome was remote and primitive, still worshiping the ancient mother goddess Ungit, and had been little changed by the civilization of Greece. Her father was a rough, crude chieftain; his passion was the hunt. By the standards of that time he was a strong king, respected if not loved. He married again—this time a delicate, gentle princess. A slave had been brought to court, a man of Greece, and the king had appointed him to teach the arts and knowledge of Greece to his two small daughters—to "practice" on them until such time as he, the king, should beget a prince, a worthy pupil. We are given a hint that Orual's face was extremely ugly. "Learning is all she will ever be good for," said her father.

So Orual acquired a second father: a wise and gentle man, a philosopher, a rationalist, the best kind of humanist who thought he had outgrown belief in the old gods and their superstitions. The king had named him the Fox. To him the child, motherless and despised by her father, gave the devotion of both her heart and her expanding mind. Redival, her younger sister, however, deprived now not only of her mother but of her sister's attention as well, and delivered over to a crude and self-seeking nurse, grew up with nothing to love but her own pretty face.

The collective consciousness of the surrounding culture was in process of emerging from a primitive identity with the unconscious, the goddess Ungit. In the coming of the Fox, we feel the penetration of the light of consciousness into the darkness of Ungit, and the king himself came to depend more and more on the Fox's clear thinking.

The king's contempt for women and for his daughters demonstrates, as always, the negative side of man's struggle to free himself from the devouring aspect of the feminine unconscious, of the mother goddess. There is no true human woman in Orual's environment. The mother is dead, the stepmother is so weak she only lives a year. The nurse is out for what she can get. The absence of eros is seen in the wild rages of the king, in the greed of Batta the nurse, in the vanity of Redival, in the superstitions into which the worship of the mother goddess is deteriorating during this time of transition. The Fox is truly kind and human, but he too misses the significance of the feminine. His way, with its rejection of the gods by the reasoning mind, is seen clearly as powerless to control the forces of barbarism.

Yet into the discord and decay at the court of Glome, as always at such moments of tension, the true miracle comes—the birth of the redeeming child. Historically, this was represented by the coming of the Buddha and the Christ; in mythology, by the dying and resurrecting of the gods; in legend, by the Grail hero and so many others; in individuals, by the intuition of redemption. All are born in such times. But in this story, in contrast to all those myths and legends, the child is a girl child, whose name is Psyche. The repressed feminine psyche is reborn as a great new possibility of redemption and transformation, which can only grow to conscious maturity in a new kind of woman who, like Orual, has learned the way of Logos and, at great cost, has held or returned to her own feminine devotion to eros.

The fury of the king on the birth of another girl was murderous. In his rage he actually stabbed to death a young boy who carried a cup of wine to him, and swore he would send the Fox to work in the mines. His contempt for the feminine not only breaks the cup and spills the wine; it also kills the boy, the promise of growing manhood, who offered the cup, and, further, it seeks to banish the bringer of the new light of reason and humanity down underground. The king's wife has died giving birth to the child. The king's hope of sons to carry on *his* way has gone; yet, in spite of his rage, his unconscious recognized the newborn child, for he called her Istra, which in Greek is Psyche.

The child had a kind of beauty that caused even the Fox in his rationalism to speak of the divine. To Orual she brought a joy beyond anything she had dreamed of. Still a child herself, she became overnight a mother to the new baby. She found a peasant woman to suckle the child and spent days and nights rejoicing in the beauty and innocence of Psyche. It was not just physical beauty; it was beauty in all its aspects.

After the ominous scene at the birth of Psyche, the years passed in deceptive peace. The king ignored his daughters; he relied more and more on the Fox in his affairs but continued on his unconscious way. Redival started a secret love affair with an officer of the guard; the king discovered them, had the young man castrated on the spot, and sold him as a eunuch slave (again it is growing young manhood that is destroyed). He blamed the Fox and Orual and ordered them to keep Redival with them always. Then one day Redival struck Psyche, and Orual's fury was such that she almost strangled Redival and had to be pulled off by the Fox.

All of Redival's values centered on her physical appearance and on her attractiveness to men, so she can be seen as a projection of Orual's shadow side. Redival was fiercely jealous of Psyche. We see later that Orual, while despising Redival's vanity and meanness, displayed these buried qualities in herself. She could not stand the ugliness of her own face and covered it with a veil—thus showing her overvaluation of superficial appearances, her refusal to face herself as she was. Her love for Psyche was so jealous a love that when in danger of losing her she dealt Psyche a blow far more deadly than any Redival could have struck. For the moment the Fox's rational arguments and tolerance could simulate peace, but the storm was brewing.

The year after Orual's fight with her sister brought the first of the bad harvests and also the first sign that the common people were beginning to identify Psyche as a goddess. People were dying like flies, and the sick began to call for Psyche to heal them, having heard that she had once nursed the Fox back to health.

The people thronged to the gates of the palace, projecting onto Psyche the divine power of innocence to heal, and the king sent her out among the sick, for he would do anything to avert a threat to himself and his power. She gave of herself wholly, and her absolute devotion brought healing, as that kind of innocence always does, but she caught the fever herself, and later in the city more and more people died. Such mass projection, as usual, turned into its opposite, and Psyche was now called the Accursed and held to be the cause of the famine and sickness. And the people threatened the palace, demanding bread.

Meanwhile the priest of Ungit himself had become ill with the fever and was for long inactive, but Redival in her malice carried news of Psyche's "deification" to him. The priest recovered and met with the leaders of the people, who reported that the "Shadowbrute" had been seen in the land: the dark god who demanded human sacrifice. The priest was of the old religion, selflessly dedicated, and he heard the voice of Ungit, the voice of the unconscious, demanding "the great offering"— the sacrifice of the best and purest in the land to the god and goddess. In the temple of Ungit he performed the ritual of the casting of lots, and the lot fell upon Psyche. She was to be given in marriage to the son of Ungit, the god who was known to many as the Shadowbrute—and to the very few as Eros. Tied to a tree far away on the holy mountain, dressed as a bride, she would be left alone for her brute lover to take.

Orual then offered to be the victim herself. The king contemptuously showed her ugly face in the mirror. She was no bride for a god. Orual's reaction seems much nobler than the king's. In terror, he resisted giving up his ego to the god. She in equal terror and blindness resisted giving up the person she most loved, which is the hardest of all sacrifices for a woman.

When Psyche herself embraced the idea of sacrifice, Orual could only feel hurt and humiliated. She felt Psyche ought to be crying on her shoulder in fear and distress; she was angry with her for this acceptance of necessity, for this faith in the meaning of her fate. Orual had always been the strong one on whom Psyche relied for all her needs, physical and emotional. She could not let go, could not rejoice in her sister's new freedom, because *she* had not set her free.

Her last words to Psyche at that parting on the eve of the sacrifice were to haunt her throughout her life. Psyche had said in her intuitive wisdom, "All my life the god of the mountain has been wooing me. O look up once at least before the end and wish me joy. . . ." Orual replied, "I only see that you have never loved me. . . . It may well be you are going to the gods. You are becoming cruel like them."

This is no remote image. It is very near to us on many levels. Countless mothers in effect do say this to their children, wives to husbands, friends to friends, when faced with another's inner growth or with separation from those they love: "You have never loved me." Moreover the highly rational educated woman of today approaches her own inmost feminine wisdom in this spirit. She, like Orual, will not allow her Psyche to connect her with the gods, with the irrational eternal paradoxes of life, with the Fool beyond reason—she sees only the cruel negative side of the sacrifice, that "making holy" of her inmost self—and she panics at the threat it brings to her determination to save the world and all the people around her through her *own* newly acquired masculine reasoning and activity. The "oughts" and "shoulds" of the animus are in fact a passionate feminine possessiveness.

This then is the great offering—the giving of that which is most loved to the god who is as yet unknown. A woman makes this offering when she is willing to risk the loss of a relationship rather than make possessive demands on the person loved. A man makes it when he will sacrifice his achievements in the world rather than betray his deeper values. To both that offering brings the experience of Eros, the god of Love.

The sacrifice then is the offering to the god of that which is most loved; it is also the end of the ego's greed. Yet this is, of course, still too rational a definition. The oneness of the best and the worst remains a mystery—for only a mystery, in the true sense of the word, redeems.

Indeed behind this mystery of the offering of the accursed and the blessed lies an even greater one—the mystery of the god who is both Love *and* the Shadowbrute. Most people, especially Christians, affirm the one truth without the other. Psyche, in the story, still young and untried, is able to look the whole reality in the face, however little she yet understands, and thereby she transcends all the rational wisdom of the Fox and accepts the unknown way she must tread: "To be eaten and to be married to the god might not be so different." For the Fox the gods are allegories of man's best qualities; for Orual they are all Shadowbrutes; therefore neither has access to the reconciling symbol of the "holy."

This paradox of the accursed and the blessed has been proclaimed in the rituals of all the religions of the world from the animal and human sacrifices of primitives to the symbolic sacrifice of the Mass; the victim had to be the best, the purest, and yet was also the scapegoat carrying the sins of the people; and always in these rituals the victim is eaten by the god and the priest, and often by all the worshipers. Thus the people were connected through the unconscious to the great paradox.

This thought returns us to our main theme—the responsibility of modern women, whose feminine values are squeezed out between the fine reasoning of the Fox and the mindless contempt of the king, to find their way back through conscious imaginative work to their intuitive awareness of the meaning of the sacrifice, and so to the "kingdom of God."

Psyche is the innermost innocence and beauty of Orual's being—that which knows but does not fully know it knows. She exists in all of us, however deeply buried under layer upon layer of ego-centered greed and one-sided conventional opinions. She is sometimes altogether forgotten and rejected; but most often in people of good will she is recognized as a great, even *the* great value, but is totally misunderstood by the conscious mind. Often she becomes an ideal pursued in all the wrong directions—either projected into the sky or onto ideas of progress or onto the people whom we love. Like Orual, we then grasp at these people or ideas with a smothering intensity, unconscious of the fact that we are at bottom holding desperately to the lost vision of our own childlike innocence. Fundamentally we are determined to cling to the *un*-conscious Paradise, to possess it forever, to refuse to the child within the agony of conscious growth. For Psyche to grow, she must be "sacrificed," and our projections must be torn away from us.

The priests then took Psyche in the ancient ritual and led her far away to the Holy Mountain and tied her to a tree. There she was abandoned. Meanwhile Orual lay for many days sick and raving in her bed. And in her dreams—a thing she could not understand—Psyche was the enemy; Psyche pursued her with jeers, and Psyche was leagued with Redival and looked like the king her father. None of this is surprising, for, as always, possessiveness contains its opposite—rejection. She had rejected her own truth, and that which we reject we meet always in dreams transformed into the enemy. Her dreams indeed foretold her life. Her double possessiveness and rejection of Psyche, and so of her own face, meant that her feminine instincts were blocked. She would find no man to love her as a woman. And so, like Tolkien's Eowyn, she took to herself the disguise of a man among men.

Still, she remained a woman, and, try as she would, she could not simply accept the Fox's reasonings as the only truth. So she fell into the most painful of all the tortures which spring from the split between the truths of the head and the truth of myth and imagination. She tried hard to believe the Fox, to live by his teaching, but, since intuitively she knew the gods existed, she saw them as wholly evil, imposing on man the most horrible cruelties just to indulge their whims. As in many women of the finest quality, the whole of her feminine unconscious turned negative.

The very day of the sacrifice, the wind changed, and very soon came rain. The plague was over; the kingdom was for the moment relieved from threats of invasion. For Orual this was a bitter joke on the part of the gods; for the Fox it was a most unfortunate coincidence tending to confirm the superstitions of the ignorant. For neither of them was there any meaning in this synchronicity; and if we refuse this meaning, we can know nothing of the inner rain whereby true grief and joy are united in a human heart. But in Orual, the woman, the refusal was a far more damaging thing than in the Fox, because of her woman's instinctive knowledge of the unconscious. She *knew* that meaning was there but refused it.

Orual was now determined to go to the mountain and bury the bones of her sister, and she persuaded Bardia, the captain of the king's guard, to go with her. As they traveled through the great silence and beauty of the fresh green land after the rain, Orual was shocked to find that her heart was tempted to dance with delight.

They arrived at the tree of sacrifice; the chains, the iron girdle hung there, but there was no trace whatever of bones, rags of clothing, or anything at all. No beast could have made so clean a sweep, no wandering shepherd would have had tools to release her. For Bardia it was no problem: the god had taken his beloved. For Orual it was a further horror undermining her rational thoughts.

They went on and down the unknown side of the mountain into the secret valley of the gods, and there on the other side of a river stood Psyche herself. Orual felt first terror, then overwhelming joy. Psyche was in rags but obviously radiant and glowing with well-being. She welcomed Orual with great delight and invited her across the stream. Together they sat and rejoiced—but only for a brief moment. Orual saw only the empty green valley, the stream, and Psyche in rags; but Psyche now told of the beautiful palace in which she lived, of the invisible hands that tended her and brought her food and wine, and of the god, who was the West Wind, who had lifted her out of her chains from the tree and brought her here, and of the greater god who had become her bridegroom, coming to lie with her at night. She was deeply happy, with only one flaw; the god had never shown himself to her. He came only in darkness and had forbidden her to make any attempt to see his face.

Orual listened in growing dismay. She could not see the palace; the wine Psyche offered her was nothing but water from the stream. When the sisters realized this difference of viewpoints, there was a terrible moment. Enmity arose between them. We see two levels of truth at war, bitterly opposed to each other. Would Psyche succumb to the "nothing but" attitude? Or would she reject Orual's truth in fury? She did neither —for already she knew intuitively the god Eros, even though she had never seen him. She accepted her sister's lack of vision with compassion.

For Orual, Psyche was either mad or deluded. But nevertheless for a brief moment she admitted that there might be things in that other dimension that she could not see.

It was at this moment of near belief that she made, in Dante's words, "the great refusal." It is a moment that comes to us all—in a dream, in an outside event or, more often, in both, when we are offered a choice—a chance to accept that unknown reality which we cannot yet see. She even had a brief vision of the towers of the palace but dismissed them as shapes in the mist. Orual refused her chance; she rejected the truth of her own psyche. She tried to force Psyche to return with her to Glome, and then recognized with anger and resentment that she no longer had any control over her young sister.

In rage she returned alone to Glome, and, reinforced by the Fox's argument that there must be a coarse, brutal man who was seducing Psyche, she traveled once more to the valley, taking with her a lamp. She was determined to persuade Psyche to disobey her lover, to light the lamp when he was asleep and look upon his face—sure that the credulous child would be disillusioned. In this plan she succeeded by a piece of blackmail so cruel that Psyche gave in. She plunged a dagger into her own arm and threatened to kill herself if Psyche would not consent. Psyche did so, but not weakly. So once more she became the great sacrifice—this time consciously for an individual person whom she loved. She was no longer the innocent victim playing a mythological role; she was a human being consciously embracing her fate.

Back across the stream Orual waited through the night. She saw the lamplight shine out across the water in the stillness—and then the calm was broken, a great voice sounded and she heard the terrible weeping of Psyche. Lightning flashed, thunder roared, and the storm tossed rocks high in the air and turned the river to a torrent. And then there came a still clear light and in it a figure with a face so beautiful and remote that she could not bear it for more than an instant; and she heard a voice "unmoved and sweet." "Now Psyche goes out in exile," it said. "Now she must hunger and thirst and tread hard roads. Those against whom I cannot fight must do their will upon her. You, woman, shall know yourself and your work. You also shall be Psyche."

It is now that the paradoxes, incredible to the reasoning mind, of the way to individuation break through to us, and we begin to sense how, without the worst in us, the best would remain in an unconscious state, unable to "know that she knows." Orual horribly betrayed her love for

Psyche; but without that betrayal Psyche herself would have continued to exist in an infantile paradise of innocence remote from human life. We have to doubt the god, insist upon seeing him, refuse to continue in childish states of projection and vague awareness, no matter what it costs. Usually we must be forced to this disobedience by the worst in ourselves. "O happy fault"—the *felix culpa* of Eve. And yet, of course, the fault remains a fault and must be paid for in full.

Orual imagined that the god's words, "You also shall be Psyche," meant that she would be exiled from Glome and wander the world hungry and homeless, like her sister. In accord with her attitude to life, she could only conceive of being punished by the gods—she could only feel that unmoved remoteness of Eros as a cold cruelty and contempt. It was impossible for her to recognize and will the necessity of the bitter separation from her own soul and the terrible loneliness it brings. Thus she did not hear what the god had actually said. For in truth he had spoken no word of condemnation; beyond all emotion, he had uttered the greatest promise any woman can hear. "You shall know yourself and your work. You also shall be Psyche." Her unconscious mind then threw up an image which her conscious mind could not grasp. His voice, she said, was like "a bird singing on the branch above a hanged man." Those who can deeply experience the joy of the bird and the horror of the hanged man as one reality have said yes to life and to the "dreadful beauty" of the god. Orual was to do so much later in her old age, but in this moment she rejected both bird and hanged man and closed her eyes to that prophecy of individuation and promise of wholeness.

Back in Glome, having refused meaning and repressed her guilt, Orual now entered upon a new way of life. Bardia had realized when she drew a sword on him, as he stood guard outside Psyche's room on the night before the sacrifice, that she had a natural skill with a weapon. Seeing her terrible grief and apathy after Psyche's going, he offered to teach her to fence, knowing in his simple way the healing power of a physical exercise which required concentration of mind and discipline of body together. Thus Orual spent many hours with him and became a first-class swordsman. It was a great turning point, for it meant she had consented to live, to fight, and to suffer. At the same time she began working hard for the king, together with the Fox, on all the business of government. Significantly, Redival—her shadow—had been consigned wholly to the care of Batta, the crude old nurse.

Thus Orual was cut off from every feminine influence or concern. Moreover she had done something crucial on her return from the hidden valley: she had put a veil over her face, which she was to wear in public for the rest of her life, until at the very end she consented to look upon her true face. Thus indeed do all women who plunge wholly into a masculine role. Having cut off their essential feminine individuality, they have no real "faces." Psyche is in exile, wandering, weeping in the unconscious, searching for Eros. Such women hide this weeping from themselves and others, but it troubles their dreams and, like Orual, they cannot shut it wholly away.

Nevertheless, now, as we read of Orual's new masculine life, we have the extraordinarily moving experience of realizing how the god's promise to Orual is at work within her. Deeper than her conscious attitudes, deeper than her bitter emotions, the true devotion and superb courage of her essential being are fundamentally in touch with the god, and so give meaning as yet unrealized to it all. She is learning to "know herself and her work" as he promised. To feel this in Orual is to realize with wonder and joy how mysterious are the patterns of our lives, in which the dark discordant threads are interwoven with those we see as bright and shining, to make at last a whole design; we recognize how blind we are in our cause-and-effect thinking, in our thin rationalistic attitudes.

The essential commitment to her love for Psyche was not shaken by her inner blindness, nor by her sin of possessiveness. She rejected that which she most loved because she could no longer own it; she rejected her own face, her own nature as woman, but she did not reject the gods themselves. She hated them; she dared to curse them for their inhumanity, which is quite a different thing from denial. It is indeed a terrific affirmation. In India, it has been said that those who hate God are considerably nearer to Him than those who love Him.

Orual's essential commitment, then, shows through in the courage with which she now set herself to do, as well as she knew how, the work that was laid upon her. She retreated behind a veil but she did not retreat from life. She thought she was working hard merely to smother her bitterness and grief, but the all-important thing was that she *worked*. She trained her body and her mind to take up the extremely heavy responsibilities that lay ahead of her. She had challenged the gods; she would not weakly cry out against her life as it was, but would make clear choices with such consciousness as she had. So her life became a story. She was not identical with her fate any longer; she related to it. The Fox's clear-sighted humanity was strong within her. She would stand on her human values and defy the gods.

The first sign of her new strength was that she was now able to face her father as an equal; never again would he strike and bully her. She felt herself equal to man on his own ground, but her contempt for herself as woman grew stronger.

As always when a new attitude emerges into consciousness, the outer events synchronized. Her father had a stroke and lay for some time mind-less and helpless. At the same moment the old priest was known to be mortally ill and the next priest took over. Orual discovered in herself her own strong masculine authority and stepped into her father's place. She astonished Bardia and the Fox by her wise judgment and her sudden independence.

It was at this juncture that Trunia, the young prince of Phars, a neighboring kingdom, took refuge at the court from the armies of his elder brother. He too was a man of tolerance and humanity, fighting to replace the old barbarism. Argan, his brother, had invaded Glome demanding the return of Trunia, and Glome, still weakened by the recent famine and plague, could not risk war. Yet to give up Trunia would equally have subjected Glome to the power of Argan, and, what was perhaps more important for Orual—still inwardly a woman as was Eowyn —it would have been an unforgivable personal betrayal. So she sent a personal challenge to Argan, proposing a duel with a champion from Glome to decide the issue. She herself would fight this duel. Bardia had told her that as a swordsman she surpassed even himself.

It was at the moment of her preparation for the fight that the king and the old priest both died. Orual was now queen, and Arnom, the new priest, was a man far more influenced by the wisdom of the Greeks, far less close to the unconscious than his predecessor. The new era was on the threshold, but all would disappear in a new barbarism if Argan were not defeated.

Orual confronted the enemy in very much the same state of mind as Eowyn. She would do her utmost to defeat the dark threat to Trunia and to her world but she half hoped she would herself be killed—for to the woman without contact with her femininity life is a weary desert. She fought and Argan was killed. Both kingdoms now had new rulers who would bring prosperity and peace to their lands in the following years.

Once again here is a woman on whose sword depended the future of her civilization. Like Eowyn, Orual wields her sword in a personal encounter which is at the same time a blow at the roots of despair. Again it has the quality of a ritual. It is also, like Eowyn's, a fight to save a single person. Unlike Eowyn, Orual wielded her sword in the wars of her country for many years after the duel, but she herself said that the only fight in which her sword achieved anything was on the one occasion when Bardia's life was in danger and she saved him. So she remained a woman at heart, and, delude herself as she might, it was basically in the cause of her love and concern for persons that she used it.

Working for many years to make sure that her victory over Argan and the forces he represented would bear fruit, Orual continued magnificently to use the sword of her masculine discrimination and authority to ensure the welfare of her people. Nevertheless because, unlike Eowyn, she continued to delude herself, continued to despise her womanhood and to refuse Psyche to the god, the devouring side of the goddess took over her emotional life. Only at the end would she realize the terrible things she had unconsciously done to the people she most loved—not only to Psyche herself, but to Bardia, to the Fox, and to Redival.

All this is made plain in the second part of the book. But there is another vital element in Orual's journey before her awakening—the experience of love and desire for a man. From the time of her first fencing lessons, Orual had realized that Bardia thought of her more and more as though she was a man—and this both grieved and pleased her. What she did not at first realize was that as a woman she was falling deeply in love with him. Some women have an extraordinary capacity for repressing this fact when they know that their love will not be returned. In Orual the full awareness of it did not break through until the moment when, after her victory in the duel, Bardia did not stay for the banquet but asked to go home as his wife was in labor, and he used the words, "Queen, the day's work is over. You'll not need me now." "I understood," said Orual, "in that moment all my father's rages." But she was not her father; she controlled her rage and was gracious. Bardia would never know what he had done to her by those words. She looked the fact in the face that she was simply "his work"—a queen, yes, but not a human woman to him, and she knew her love for him and her terrible jealousy of his wife.

This happened on the very day on which, of all others, she had been acclaimed as a hero in an exclusively masculine field of activity. She had conquered with a sword. And now, as though her unconscious would not tolerate this, she was pierced through and through as a woman by her love for Bardia. She was now to discover the agony of instinctive desire, an experience without which no man or woman can reach maturity. It is well to affirm here that, contrary to popular belief, the physical consummation of such desire is not essential to maturity. The instincts may sometimes be even more deeply experienced without that consummation, as Orual's story makes clear.

On that night of achievement and bitterness she drank too much wine at the banquet and here is her account of how she felt when she went to her lonely bed:

> My double loneliness, for Bardia, for Psyche. Not separable. The picture, the impossible fool's dream, was that all should have been different from the very beginning and he would have been my husband and Psyche our daughter. Then I would have been in labor . . . with Psyche . . . and to me he would have been coming home. But now I discovered the wonderful power of wine . . . not at all that it blotted out these sorrows—but that it made them seem glorious and noble, like sad music, and I somehow great and reverend for feeling them. I was a great, sad queen in a song. I did not check the big tears that rose in my eyes. I enjoyed them.

These last sentences reveal the negative side of the realization of one's life as a story. It is a pitfall few can avoid at one time or another. We are inflated by our own suffering and the ego identifies then with the victim of "the sacrifice." There are people who positively insist on being victims, over and over again.

Orual goes on to tell us how she heard the chains swinging in the well, the sound of which always brought to her the illusion of Psyche crying, cold and hungry, outside. Her love for Bardia and for Psyche are in fact manifestations of one love, but in her present state they are simply mixed—"not separable"—and therefore, of course, very definitely not in harmony, and this is so because Orual herself is not a woman *united* to the masculine spirit within her. She is an undifferentiated man-woman. She wants Bardia to love her as a woman, Psyche to love her as a man; and in the midst of all this her personal emotions become unendurable. How powerful is the symbolism of the chains creaking in the well—the sound of Psyche weeping which she cannot shut out! The chains are an image which brings to mind the essential bondage of the commitment of real love through which a woman draws up the water of the unconscious for man. They are creaking unused in the winds of Orual's spirit, and, meanwhile, her true psyche weeps as she searches for the god. For love brings us freedom only when we accept its binding nature: "I locked up Orual or laid her asleep as best I could somewhere deep down inside me; she lay curled there. It was like being with child, but reversed; the thing I carried in me grew slowly smaller and less alive."

The Fox grew old and died. Orual had freed him before her encounter with Argan, and she never allowed herself to realize how great was the sacrifice he had made for her sake when he decided to stay in Glome and not return to his beloved Greece. His service to her had been beyond price, but in his extreme old age his thinking grew confused; his intellect gave way to unclear images and to too much talk. It is indeed what happens to overrational thinking, especially that of the animus in women.

Meanwhile the queen locked away her memory of the god she had heard in the valley, and she thought she had almost succeeded in substituting the Fox's philosophy for all concern with the gods. Nevertheless she had to build thick stone walls around the well in the courtyard with the creaking chains, in order to shut out the weeping of Psyche.

She had two strengths, she said, in her queenship. The first was the wisdom of her two councilors, the Fox and Bardia, and the fact that they treated her like a man; her second was her veil. For this gave her an aura of mystery which carried great power. People began to notice the beauty of her voice and her figure, and to tell all sorts of stories about what lay behind the veil. It is well for us to think of how often in daily living we unconsciously use this hiding of our identity behind a veil as a kind of power mechanism. It is a different thing from the persona. When we retire behind a veil we deliberately hide our true faces, our essential attitudes and values. The persona is a necessary shield between a person and the world. At best it expresses a person's truth, while protecting him from invasion; at worst, it is a collective personality which takes over his truth or is used by him to deceive. A veil offers nothing in place of the truth. Hence its power to incur projections.

Through the years Orual necessarily met Ansit, Bardia's wife, from time to time, and jealousy tortured her. She tried to comfort herself with her knowledge of being part of his man's life, but it did not ease her; neither did the thought of Bardia's simple, wholehearted devotion to both queen and wife. She wrote, "This is what it is to be a man. The one sin the gods never forgive us is that of being born woman." How appalling a point of view this sounds to a modern woman! Yet in fact it is a deeply repressed belief which is at the root of the behavior of so many women whose values have turned masculine at the expense of their womanhood.

After the death of the Fox, Orual was restless. There was peace and prosperity in the kingdom and she decided to go on a journey through her own and neighboring lands, after which she hoped that she and Bardia could rest more and delegate the work. It was on the way back from this outer journey that the event happened which precipitated her writing her book, her complaint against the gods, and so started her inner journey to self-knowledge.

She came one day upon a little temple in the woods with a small wooden statue of a goddess whose face was covered with a veil. It was cool, clean, and light in the temple. The priest, a quiet old man, came to speak to her and she asked about the goddess. He replied that she was a very young goddess whose name was Istra. And he told her then the sacred story of Psyche and Eros, as it has been told through the centuries. As Orual listened to her own story, as she thought, she grew more and more angry at what she called the half-truths. Most of all she exclaimed against the statement that the two ugly sisters in the story had *seen* the palace in the valley. "But why did she—they—want to separate her from the god, if they had seen the palace?" They wanted, said the priest, to destroy her *because* they had seen the palace and were jealous. Instantly Orual resolved to write her book. She would tell the real story and expose the lie that she had seen the palace. She could shut out the gods no longer; she would face them and tell the truth about the cruelty: "I could never be at peace again until I had written my charge against the gods. It burned me from within. It quickened; I was with book, as a woman is with child." Through her book, the child which was her true self was conceived and would in due time come to birth and maturity.

A dream came to her at this time. It reproduced the first task of Psyche in the myth—the sorting of the seeds. In it she sat before an immense pile of mixed seeds which must be sorted before morning. Failure would bring disaster, and she knew in her dream that success was humanly impossible. Near despair, she nevertheless set to work—and then in her dream she saw herself as a tiny ant carrying a seed on her back and staggering under the weight of it. Not until the end was she to realize that it was the work of the ants which enabled Psyche to succeed.

Her book was, of course, the sorting of the seeds—the immensely painful task of discrimination, of complete honesty, as far as she was capable of it, about the thoughts, feelings, and actions of her life. It is the first necessity of the way to consciousness for women.

Thus the first part of her book was written; only after that came the brief fifty pages in which Orual's transformation breaks through into her life. The change begins with the first real encounter on equal terms that she had ever had in her life with a truly feminine woman.

Bardia was dead. He had been sick for a while, but it seemed not a serious thing except that he had no strength to rally from it and gradually weakened and died. Orual, overwhelmed with grief, went to visit Ansit, Bardia's widow, with bitter jealousy in her heart, but trying to accept the other's sorrow. She spoke to Ansit of Bardia's seemingly light sickness, and then the formalities between them crumbled. Ansit told of her bitterness—of how Bardia's strength had been slowly eaten away by the weight of the responsibilities which the queen had laid upon him, by the demands upon his time and attention year after year, by day and by night. And she, Ansit, had waited for the short times he could spend at home, had watched his weariness, his unflinching loyalty to the queen. At first Orual defended herself. Ansit had had all—husband, children— she nothing. "I'll not deny it," said Ansit. "I had what you left of him."

At this Orual lifted her veil. It was a turning point in her life. She stood exposed and face to face with the woman who was her enemy. "Are you jealous of this?" she asked; and Ansit, looking into Orual's true face, into her eyes, recognized for a moment the love and suffering there. "You loved him. You've suffered, too." They wept for a few blessed moments in each other's arms.

The moment could not last. Each regressed into her own shadow side again; Orual resumed her veil, Ansit her bitterness. Orual spoke again. "You made me little better than the Lord Bardia's murderer . . . did you believe what you said?"

"Believe? I do not believe, I know that your queenship drank up his blood year by year and ate out his life." Ansit still differentiates between the suffering woman and the queen.

Orual had succeeded all too well in her aim after her rejection of Psyche and the god—her aim which was, as she had written it, "to build up more and more that strength, hard and joyless, which had come to me when I heard the god's sentence; by learning, fighting, and laboring, to drive all the woman out of me." The natural joy in being a woman, repressed into the unconscious, drinks the blood, eats the life out of those around such a woman.

Ansit then says, "Oh, Queen Orual, I begin to think you know nothing of love. Or no; I'll not say that. Yours is Queen's love, not commoners'. Perhaps you who spring from the gods love like the gods. Like the

Shadowbrute. They say the loving and the devouring are all one, don't they?"

Here is the great irony! Orual's whole adult life had been lived in bitter rebellion against just those words spoken by Psyche before her sacrifice: "To be eaten and to be married to the god might not be so different." Orual had cried out in fury that the love of the gods was nothing but horrible cruelty. And now out of the mouth of the human woman whom Bardia had loved came the same words applied to her own love. She herself is the one who has loved with the cruelty of the gods. Because she was unable to accept that the vision of Eros in his true form included the Shadowbrute, the devouring and the being devoured, she was doomed to live out these things unconsciously, split off from her conscious love. She would have bitterly rejected the words of St. Ignatius of Antioch on the way to the arena: "Let me be ground by the teeth of the wild beasts that I may be found a true bread." For St. Ignatius the beast was as true a manifestation of the divine as the angel. He had his levels clear. A terrible cruelty on one level did not destroy for him the beauty of the bird singing beside the hanged man.

Orual has come to her second great moment of choice. Ansit, though mature where Orual was unconscious, was weak where Orual was strong. She fell into a cruel personal bitterness, and her last words to Orual were, "You're full fed. Gorged with other men's lives, women's too: Bardia's, mine, the Fox's, your sisters'—both your sisters." Orual, though filled with a blinding fury in which she, the queen, could have delivered Ansit over to torture and death, in reprisal, did not give in to her instinctual rage. Her long discipline and her love of human justice bore fruit; but even these things would not have been enough, if she had not been touched at last by that other dimension of truth which she had so often rejected. For the first time she was able to say, "Something (if it was the gods, I bless their name) made me unable to do this"—and in a few days' time she knew "those divine Surgeons had me tied down and were at work . . . it was all true—truer than Ansit could know."

Ansit's words were, of course, only one side of the double truth, but because Orual had refused the knowledge of it for so long she had to experience it first as the only truth. In the hours and nights that followed she faced the horror of looking on that which she had called love and seeing only its other face—the hatred which had poisoned it from first to last.

During the long process of the purging of love we all must come to know the empty desert which accompanies the death of a craving which we recognize at last for what it is. How much in all our loves is a demand to be fed by other people's lives—not an acceptance of food freely given? Those men and women who give their lives consciously to be "eaten" without thought of return are indeed fed by the god within, but Orual was gorged and starving.

That which came to her in one stark moment of truth comes more often to us in smaller moments of insight interspersed with regressions; for we cannot at first stand the sense of nothingness for long, and we hasten to fill it with new cravings. In Orual's story, however, we see the lifelong process with great clarity, condensed into a few years, or months, perhaps, at the end of her life. She has become, she says, "a gap"—and only in that gap can the divine surgeons do their work. It is important to realize the quality of her disillusionment, since it is so very easy for us to confuse the real experience with the absolutely opposite experience of self-disgust which can delude us by simulating the emptiness. The latter merely drives us into a despairing guilt which is the opposite face of our ego pride. Self-justification and escape inevitably follow.

The three words which tell us that Orual has truly accepted the bitter truth are in parentheses. "My love for Bardia (not Bardia himself) had become to me a sickening thing." "Not Bardia himself." The self-disgust which simulates the true facing of the shadow never brings such a clear distinction between the craving and the thing craved for, however much we may cover up this fact—"It is all my fault" we say, usually meaning just the opposite. The three words tell us that Orual for the first time is seeing Bardia as separate from herself—as his own man, not as her possession, and it is this that guarantees her honesty and gives her strength to stay still in the emptiness.

The shock which awakened Orual had come from an outer event, and, because she accepted this bitter fact with the whole of herself as far as she yet knew that self, the drama now moved into the inner world and the gods began to speak to her "face to face" in a series of great dreams and visions which completed her life and showed her the vision of immortality. She began not simply to recognize facts but to know the truth which comes only with the awakening of the creative imagination.

We, for the most part, experience the shocks and visions alternately, working for long years outwardly and inwardly to recognize the myth and the meaning. Yet surely it often happens in Orual's way, perhaps more frequently than we realize. She had spent most of the years of her life in an inner hell of her own making, and she was quite unaware of the purgation which she passed through at the same time, nor did she realize the real significance of her book. The breakthrough of vision, of consciousness, which now came to her before her death took place in the space of a very few weeks. The timing is after all not important, for life is a circle, a sphere, and will be known as such only when we have wholly accepted the straight lines of time and mortality.

The process of individuation was now forcing itself up into Orual's consciousness. She felt stripped of everything, but still she clung desperately to the last fortress of her egocentricity. She asserted vehemently that she had truly loved Psyche, that in this one thing she had been blameless, had suffered terrible injustice from the gods. We each have a last fortress of this kind—"in this one thing at least," we tell ourselves, "I have been wholly blameless, all good." Over and over again the cry is heard, "Why do I make no progress when I long so sincerely to grow?" The answer of course is that the longing is still, like Orual's, a demand to possess. There is no progress *toward* wholeness—only a preparation for death and rebirth.

We come now to a final great vision in which Orual is brought to the ultimate stripping—to the death before death in which at last she is unmade and recreated. The god's prophecy is about to be fulfilled: she will know herself as Psyche while at the same time she remains uniquely and forever Orual.

She knew with certainty that the vision was not a dream. It included her conscious self, like the "active imagination" of Jung's terminology. It began with her setting forth over a parched desert, knowing she must find the water of death and bring it to Ungit. Orual thought she was carrying a bowl as she labored on for, it seemed, hundreds of years, her throat parched with terrible thirst. Sometimes the sand rose over her ankles and all the time the pitiless sun beat down from exactly overhead so that she cast no shadow; there were no shadows at all. It is a terrifying image of the life of consciousness cut off entirely from the unconscious, from the darkness and mystery of life, from the waters which bring death and healing, but Orual was at last truly searching for the waters though still unaware of their meaning or of the nature of her true goal. Her thirst was now so desperate that she would drink of any water, however bitter; she longed simply for relief from the terrible sunlight. But she came only to a new horror, to unscalable mountains crawling with serpents and scorpions, and in the heart of these mountains, she knew, lay the well of water that she sought.

She had come to the end of any possible effort, sitting on the burning sands. She was at the meeting place of opposites, for the cold-blooded instinctive poison of snake and scorpion is at the opposite pole from the burning aridity of one-sided intellect. There came now a shadow in the sky, and Orual prayed that it might be a cloud, a blessed cloud bringing rain. But it was not. Then, "though the terrible light seemed to bore through my eyeballs into my brain," she saw that the small dark shape was an eagle, a great eagle of the gods, and it came to rest beside her.

To remember the symbolism of the eagle at this point greatly enhances the impact of the vision. The eagle is the messenger of the gods; he is an image of the true spirit soaring above the earth, yet resting upon it, and casting a blessed shadow. He redeems from the autonomous intellect, from the pride of man's spirit cut off from the shadows and from the waters of the unconscious. For Charles Williams, Tolkien, and Lewis, all three, the eagle was the savior in man's extremity of need.

He comes to each one, it seems, only when every possible effort of which the ego is capable has been made. It was he who took Psyche's bowl, in the myth, when she was about to despair, and brought to her the water of death. To Orual he now came at last, but he could bring no water because, as she now discovered to her horror, she carried in her hands not a bowl but a book—the book in which she had written her complaint against the gods.

All Orual's hopes fell in ruins about her. Yet in reading what follows we feel an extraordinary excitement. Far from rebuking her and casting her away, the great bird cried out as it were in joy. "She's come at last . . . the woman who has a complaint against the gods." The spirit in a woman such as Orual, who has lived by the masculine principle, cannot bring her the water she seeks, but nevertheless because of her long devotion and suffering he can and does lead her to the experience through which she will find her bowl, her womanhood, again. It is as though the masculine spirit itself rejoices in the coming of this new woman to her great moment.

At the eagle's voice the souls of the dead rise out of the mountain to greet her. They are buried images of her ancestors, her heritage, the gathered experiences of humanity itself: "Here is the woman. Bring her in. Bring her into court. . . . To the judge, to the judge." She cannot yet find the water, but she who has loved and served human justice has found the place of ultimate justice.

The great image of the eagle in Dante symbolized above all else divine justice. In the great eagle of souls in the Heaven of Jupiter, all speak with one voice but the voice proceeds not from a collective "we" but from a thousand "I's" in the final unity of judgment which is not a choice between this and that but a recognition of the whole.

Justice is the greatest manifestation of the Logos principle on earth, and the hardest thing for the feminine psyche to learn. Orual sought it with all the energies of her mind and heart, and in doing so exclusively she lost her feminine instinctive roots, and therefore her vision of the nature of the divine. In this moment of Orual's story when we hear the eagle's glad cry, "She's come . . . the woman who has a complaint against the gods," we realize that what such a woman has sought with the devotion of her whole being she finds (for what we wholly seek we inevitably find); and that when she recognizes and accepts its logic in her own life at last, it will be to her the opening of the door to all that she has rejected. She will know the true nature of mercy and love.

Orual was seized upon by many hands, pushing her, lifting her toward a great hole in the heart of the mountain. She was plunged into the cold and dark out of the burning light and found herself alone, standing on a rock, while around her in a gray light a sea of faces—thousands upon thousands of the souls of the dead—stretched away out of her sight. Near her feet were the faces of her own dead—the Fox, her father, Batta, Argan—and far away there was a veiled figure cloaked in black (whether male or female she could not tell) sitting on a rock raised above the others. It was the judge; and he spoke saying, "Uncover her." Hands reached up and stripped off her veil and every stitch of clothing, leaving her old body and her Ungit face exposed to the vast concourse of souls. Only her book remained in her hand, and it was small and tattered—not at all like the great book she felt she had written. "No thread to cover me, no bowl in my hand to hold the water of death, only my book."

"Read your complaint," said the judge. Another agonizing and final choice was before her, and she almost yielded to the last temptation. Seeing the poor shabby thing she held, she thought she would fling it down and trample on it—tell them her true work had been stolen. And as she unrolled the parchment and saw the mean and vile scribble—a writing so unlike her own—she wanted desperately to repudiate her work, to deny that it was truly hers and refuse to read it.

It is a moment of great danger. When the time comes that we are stripped to the bone and suddenly it appears to us how poor and shabby is the work we have done into which we have poured all that we thought best and purest in us, then indeed we may feel an overwhelming temptation to betray our own truth. We cannot stand the exposure of our despicable pride and so we long to deny responsibility for our own story for what we are, good or bad, right or wrong.

"Whatever they do to me, I will never read out this stuff," thought Orual. "But already I heard myself reading it." She was ready in her depths to accept the whole truth in spite of shame and disillusionment, ready to let go of her last fortress of pride and possessiveness.

So she laid bare the whole of her complaint against the gods—the ultimate protest of human rationality and ugly possessive love:

You'll say I was jealous. Jealous of Psyche? Not while she was mine. If
you'd gone the other way to work—if it was my eyes you had opened—
you'd soon have seen how I would have shown her and told her and
taught her and led her up to my level. . . . There should be no gods at
all, there's our misery and bitter wrong. . . . We want to be our
own.[Italics added.] I was my own and Psyche was mine and no
one else had any right to her. Oh, you'll say you took her away
into bliss and joy such as I could never have given her, and I ought
to have been glad of it for her sake. Why? What should I care for
some horrible, new happiness which I hadn't given her and which
separated her from me? Do you think I wanted her to be happy,
that way? . . . She was mine. *Mine.* . . .

"Enough," said the judge at last. Silence fell; and Orual knew that she
had been reading the same thing over and over again. Suddenly she
heard her voice strange to her ears: "There was given to me a certainty
that this, at last, was my own voice." All projection was at an end. Never
again could blame be laid on anyone, any circumstance, any god. The
silence was long and profound. At last the judge spoke. "Are you answered?" "Yes," said Orual.

We have arrived at the last chapter. It begins with the words I quoted
at the beginning: "The complaint was the answer. To have heard myself
making it was to be answered." This is the inexorable justice of the god.
Our thinking may long have outgrown the projected image of an avenging god meting out rewards and punishments from his judgment seat; and
yet the attitude remains in the unconscious as powerful as ever, because
our thinking has not encompassed the true nature of justice. To be in hell
is to refuse the tension of the opposites and therefore all self-knowledge;
to be in purgatory is to accept that tension and to enter the long struggle
for the knowledge of who we are, a struggle which involves the passionate integrity whereby we stand by our own truth even against the gods on
whatever level of awareness we may be. The emergence from purgatory
into the heaven of wholeness will come, as it did to Statius in the *Divine*
Comedy, and as it came to Orual in the place of judgment, when we have

suffered the tension long enough and deeply enough to find ourselves suddenly through and beyond it as we hear and accept our own voices, our own faces, exactly as they are.

Orual did not yet know what had happened. It was no great emotional experience of new insight. She knew only that her complaint was finally answered because she had at last *heard* it. Still with her rational mind she expected judgment and punishment—but *this* trial was over. She had accused the gods and was answered. She had been the plaintiff; it remained, she thought, for the gods to accuse her, for she was still unaware of the nature of the divine mercy.

This then is the woman's test: to go straight to the goal of her spirit against all the deepest feminine instincts. The crucial test of the man is exactly the opposite. Will he respond to the promptings of the heart and turn aside from his goals to help another in need? If he does not do so he is lost. It is not, however, so simple an issue for modern men and women halfway to the realization of the contrasexual principle in themselves. Each has a double test, for the animus must learn compassion and the anima must find strength to emerge from the moods which so easily turn the man aside from his way. Orual understood now how she herself, the woman who refused the way of all women and who mistook the meaning of the new masculine strength she felt in herself, had almost wrecked Psyche's chance of wholeness. Her animus had set for her a rational, opinionated goal and held to it, shutting out compassion but demanding it from others. Nevertheless deep down in her unconscious her true feminine psyche was true to her way because, no matter how distorted, Orual's love was a true love at its root, and her quest was for truth at all costs.

Orual had at last understood the whole of Psyche's myth and had seen the pattern of her own life within it. She accepted every last shred of responsibility for her own story and it was almost time now for her final realization.

But first, there is another aspect here which raises a deep question. In almost all fairy stories and novels of the Christian Era until very recent times, the transforming love in human beings has been heterosexual. For two thousand years our one-sided drive for ego consciousness and the resultant eclipse of the feminine has caused the love of man for man, which presupposes a feminine element in the male, to be regarded as criminal, while the love of woman for woman has been for the most part simply ignored as insignificant. When Radclyffe Hall wrote *The Well of Loneliness* at the beginning of the twentieth century, the collective reaction of horror was extreme. We may find this strange today, when these things are openly discussed, and novels such as those of Mary Renault are accorded the high praise they deserve. But free intellectual discussion and even the creative imagination of the few are very far from the perception of meaning by the general public. There is a long way to go before love—love, not lust—between persons of the same sex is accepted and respected to the same degree as heterosexual love. Any love, for anyone, if it goes deep enough may be the way to transformation. The extraordinary interest of Lewis's myth in this context lies in the fact that Orual is a woman with normal heterosexual instincts, whose deepest love is nevertheless given to a woman. Though she truly loves and desires Bardia, Psyche is her heart's beloved. Tentatively I would ask whether this does not point to a little-recognized inner truth for women of today who are seeking individuation.

Any person of insight would surely agree that, if a woman or a man is unable to relate satisfactorily to others of the same sex, it is proof of a state of undifferentiated consciousness. But the love of Orual for Psyche points at something more powerful than the capacity for this kind of relatedness. It is *through* her love for a woman that she finds at last the reconciling symbol and is united to the god.

It is, I believe, true that for a woman who has a strong androgynous nature her love for another woman can sometimes lift her to greater heights and plunge her into deeper pain than her love for a man. There is certainly no question about this in the case of Orual's two great loves. It can be, in fact, a deeply religious experience when the symbolic meaning breaks through.

It is easy to explain these things in terms of mother and father complexes and so on, and end up by killing the potential beauty of such relationships. The emergence of the contrasexual element in both men and women in this age will increasingly mean that a maturing person will know love for both sexes. The experience of love and desire between persons of the same sex need not necessarily include a physical outlet—indeed the release of tension on the physical level, since it is symbolically devoid of potential creativity, may destroy the meaning of the experience in such relationships. As with all new shoots of consciousness, however, the dangers of misunderstanding and misplacement of levels are very great. These things belong to the secret life of the individual in whom, through love—to repeat Jung's words—"the fire of suffering" will melt those "incompatible substances, the male and the female," until the goal of life is known in the *hierosgamos* of Psyche, the human being, and Eros, the god.

I have never felt altogether at ease with the statement we so often read in Jungian books that the symbol of the Self appears to us usually as someone of our own sex. It can be misleading. Psyche in the story is not in herself a symbol of the Self even at the end; neither is Eros. God though he is, he is still under the domination of the mother—imprisoned in the unconscious—until the human Psyche has done her part. Then *he* becomes incarnate and *she* is lifted up to the divine. The true symbol of the Self is always a union of opposites. It is clearer perhaps to say that we may first glimpse the Self through an androgynous image of our own sex. Therefore, while we project the image of the animus or anima onto the opposite sex, we are apt to project the Self onto our own, and it is this that makes love for someone of our own sex extremely dangerous as well as an intensely creative opportunity. On the one hand it can become autoeroticism and lead to a deadly kind of possession through identification with the archetype—a thing which kills all true human feeling; on the other it can become the experience which leads through the purging of our possessiveness to the vision of the *hierosgamos*.

Orual's love for Psyche, both the danger, which almost destroyed her, and the transformation which it wrought in her, are clear before us in unforgettable images. Hard as was her awakening to the greed of her love for Bardia, it was far harder for her to let go of her possessive love for Psyche, who was an image of her very self.

There is, however, a great difference between the love of a woman for a woman and that of a man for a man, a difference which derives first from the mystery of the mother-daughter relationship, as with Demeter and Kore, and second from the differing natures of the animus and the anima. Irene de Castillejo has written of this last fact, which is too little stressed in Jungian thought. She points out that the animus is very different in its function from the anima, in that the anima *is* in a sense his experience of the feminine unconscious, whereas the animus is the image who enables a woman to differentiate herself *from* the eternally feminine unconscious. In its negative form, of course, the animus cuts the woman off from this, while the negative anima simply drags a man into it. The point is that the inspiration, the numinous ground of the unconscious to which the masculine gives form, in either man or woman, is feminine.

May Sarton, in her novel *Mrs. Stevens Hears the Mermaids Singing*, has written of this same thing. Mrs. Stevens is an old woman who is a well-known poet. In the book she is interviewed by a young man and woman for the press, and she looks back over her whole life. As she does so she realizes that, much as she has owed to the men she has loved, the inspiration of her creative spirit did not come from them. It sprang rather from her passionate loves for a few women, from her childhood onward, and from the suffering and joy that such loving brought her. The Muses, she rightly concludes, are feminine, not only for men but for women also. Sappho, that very great woman poet, was likewise a lover of women.

A woman must hear the mermaids' song from the sea if she is to make contact with her creative imagination. When she has heard it, then the work of the animus begins—the hard work of bringing to focus, defining, giving expression to that song from her feminine depths.

We have now reached the moment in Orual's story when she is about to meet her beloved again:

> Now I knew that she was a goddess indeed. Her hands burned me (a painless burning) when they met mine. The air that came from her clothes and limbs and hair was wild and sweet; youth seemed to come into my breast as I breathed it. And yet . . . with all this, even because of all this, she was the old Psyche still; a thousand times more her very self than she had been before the Offering. For all that had then but flashed out in a glance or a gesture, all that one meant most when one

spoke her name, was now wholly present, not to be gathered up from
hints nor in shreds, not some of it in one moment and some in another.
Goddess? I had never seen a real woman before.

Orual was silent in the fullness of her joy. But it was not the end:
"Suddenly . . . I knew that all this had been only a preparation. Some
far greater matter was upon us." She heard again unseen voices. "He is
coming," they said. "The god is coming into his house. The god comes to
judge Orual."

No joy without terror; no beauty without dread—Orual knew it now
as the arrows of the god pierced her through and through. She was
standing beside Psyche at the edge of the water, the water transfigured by
fire. She cast down her eyes and saw—not her old ugly face beside
Psyche's beauty, as in the old king's mirror. She saw in the mirror of the
water of life and death two Psyches, both "beautiful beyond all imagining"—though it no longer mattered in those terms—the same and yet
not the same, for still, though "unmade" and recreated, still she was
Orual.

Then came the great voice once more. "You also are Psyche," it said.
This was the final judgment. This time it was no distant promise; it was
eternal reality, and as she heard it Orual had courage to raise her eyes
and she saw—gloriously and finally she saw—no god and no pillared
court but her own garden and her own book in her human hand, the
simple daily realities of her life, transformed now by the union of Psyche
with the god.

Orual knew that she was very near to her physical death and was
content. Her circle was complete. Touchingly she wondered why those
around her should weep for her when she had done so little to give them
cause to love her. She died as she wrote the last sentence of her story.

There is a brief epilogue written by Arnom, the priest: "This book was
all written by Queen Orual of Glome, who was the most wise, just,
valiant, fortunate and merciful of all the princes known in our parts of
the world." She was indeed a great prince in spirit, and in the end a great
and simple human woman, whole and complete.

PART

IV

A FREEDOM TO BE ONESELF

Note: This interview, conducted by Barbara Rotz, originally in *Anima: The Journal of Human Experience*.

ANIMA   Could you share a little of your personal history? I know you originally studied French and Italian literature at Oxford University. What led you to become interested in the writings of Jung?

HELEN LUKE   Oh yes, I could tell you about that. It was quite dramatic. It was during World War II. I had two small sons and my husband worked in London where he was an administrative civil servant. I had taken the boys away to a little cottage by the sea, where it was somewhat safe for that time, for a holiday.

A friend of mine who was in Jungian analysis—I didn't know a thing about it and had never read about Jung—lent me a little book. It was about somebody whose dream was interpreted in a Jungian way. I was absolutely stunned by this interpretation and with the realization that dreams could mean anything.

Anyway, I remember going to bed and reading and reading—there was only candlelight—and then going to sleep and having a dream. In this dream, I was going down and down until I hit bottom, as though I had died almost. Then I started coming up again saying, "Now I shall know! Now I shall know!" And I understood it was this book that was going to change my whole life.

When I got home from the holiday I found that my husband had bought me a copy of what was called in those days *The Psychology of the Unconscious*—one of Jung's most difficult books. It was the only time in my life I have literally sat up all night reading. I couldn't stop. It was as though I recognized, "This is something I've always known. I don't understand a word of it, but I know it."

Very soon after that, the friend who had lent me the book said, "I've made an appointment for you with my analyst. You asked me to." I replied that I certainly had never asked her any such thing! I was sure that her analyst never took anybody except artists and people like that and she wouldn't look at me. But my friend said, "You asked me to! I've made a date for you." So I went up to London and had an hour with her, and that was it.

ANIMA   What a fascinating series of events! Did you begin your training in Jungian analysis at that time?

H.L.   Yes. After the war ended, my analyst sent me to Zurich. I was in Zurich for the first semester of the newly created Training Institute—the very thing Jung had not wanted but which he decided to go along with because, perhaps, he could have some influence. Jung was skeptical of setting up a big structure. Not that he was against the Jung Club where they had lectures and seminars. They were small things, you see. But this was a whole big structure.

ANIMA   Jung probably understood the dangers of institutionalizing anything. Eventually it gets tied up in bureaucracy and power play.

H.L.   Yes, that's right. Anyway, I worked with Dr. Meier, who was the first head of the Institute and a friend of Jung's. I had just six months because that's all I could afford and all the time I had.

I was also granted one hour with Jung. Jung had retired, of course, but Dr. Meier got me an hour with him. I was a little annoyed when Dr. Jung began talking about the difference between American and European patients. I wanted to talk about myself! That's the way he was in his old age. But whatever he talked about turned out to be of great value to the listener. Jung talked about three things, all of which became vitally important in the next year or two of my life. That was the beginning.

ANIMA   That was the beginning of your studies . . .

H.L.   I didn't, by the way, finish the official course. I continued studying with my original analyst and began work with clients in London. Later I had a chance to go to America. My marriage had ended at that time, but in a positive way as you may have gathered from some of my writing. [See "The Marriage Vow," p. 63.] And that's how life here began.

ANIMA   This was a time of tremendous change and turning. Your life was affected at all levels, wasn't it?

H.L.   Yes, indeed. I had an experience in a dream at that time which told me very clearly that I would never be able to train or work through any collective institutional structure but I had to journey on a quiet and lonely way. In the years that followed, the meaning of this dream became clearer and clearer. Every time I forgot it, as I did from time to time, and tried to connect with an institution, something always happened to make it impossible. No, my way was to be alone, but in relationship with others of like mind.

ANIMA   When you came to the United States you settled in Los Angeles. How did your experiences in California lead to your decision to establish a self-styled community in rural Michigan? Did the concept of Apple Farm begin while you were working there?

H.L.   The seed of Apple Farm was sown there. I worked as a counselor for twelve years in partnership with a friend and with the support of a few other analysts. Some of us always had a feeling that we wanted to establish a little group where people could come who couldn't afford the large sums it costs to do an analysis or for whom that wasn't really necessary. We understood that some people just needed to talk with others who had long experience of dreams and the inner life and who could help them discover how to have a dialogue with their inner selves.

ANIMA   How did this understanding translate into Apple Farm? Did you establish a formal program or just make yourselves available to those who wished to explore the realms of the inner self?

H.L.   We have been asked to explain what we do here and it's almost impossible to put it into words. People talk individually to one of us, and then we have one discussion group with the guests each week. Almost everybody who stays—even within hours of being here—feels an atmosphere of absolute freedom to be themselves. We can't say how that happens except that we try to live it. We can't really explain what goes on. One guest described her visit afterward in these words: "One meets individuals, breathing free air, finding their own way."

We are not, in the ordinary sense, a community. There are no rules. There are no conditions or pledges. Everyone is bound together by a basic commitment to finding who they are; what they are born to be, which is the meaning of Jung's word "individuation."

ANIMA   As I read your book *Kaleidoscope* I was intrigued by your references to the feminist movement. You are clearly frustrated with some aspects of that movement. Recently I have felt that we are entering what might be called a postfeminist age . . .

H.L.   I agree. It's coming, I hope as you say, a post*feminist*, not a post*feminine* age.

ANIMA   Do you think this new phase will address some of your concerns? I know you have some strong feelings about what the feminist movement has done to some women.

H . L .   Yes, it turned some into imitation men. Have you read my book *Woman: Earth, and Spirit?* In that I go into the whole thing about women's contempt for their own principles and femininity.

A N I M A   Could you talk about this? I think our readers would be very interested in what you mean by women's contempt for their own principles.

H . L .   A lot of what the women's movement has done is wonderful. But a negative result can come to many women when they are obsessed with a deep resentment against the patriarchy. This resentment creates a need, not just to discover and live the talents they had been forbidden to develop, but to imitate the masculine approach to life. Therefore they tend to look with contempt on the beautiful and basic values of giving birth, of nurturing and caring, and foremost of all values, that of learning how to love.

A N I M A   On the one hand these women say they don't like how men have handled things, but then they turn around and try to be just like them. So theirs is really a contempt for their own feminine values, not the masculine values.

H . L .   Exactly. Just like people who go on resenting what happened to them in childhood as though they weren't responsible for their own lives when they grow up.

A N I M A   How do you understand feminine principles? Is it possible to define them in a way that speaks to both men and women? Clearly the feminine is of value to both.

H . L .   It is interesting that there's an old goddess of Buddhism called Tara. Her name is derived from two Sanskrit words meaning "savior" and "star." I talked about that at our Christmas Eve party this year. I thought that was a beautiful Eastern name for the Mary within us, who is, for

Christians, the Intercessor—from the Latin *intercedere* meaning "to yield between." That is the feminine. She stands between.

I like to think of it, in Christian terms, as God the Father, God the Son, and the Holy Spirit who is the wisdom and the love between creator and created. The Holy Ghost is both masculine and feminine, if you like, but largely a very feminine thing—that *which is between*. I find the most beautiful thought in any relationship between two people that goes deep is that it isn't just the egos—the two egos—that are involved. It is the two selves and they only meet when you awaken that which is between and which finally brings about unity.

ANIMA   What does this say about the efforts of the women's movement in the last twenty years?

H . L .   When I speak of where the feminist movement does belong, I speak from the experience of my early life. My mother was a very active suffragette in pre–World War I England. At that time women were fighting for the basic rights of the vote, owning their own property, being allowed to work on equal terms with men. This is quite a different thing from what became, in our time, a sense of wanting to change the woman's nature into the same mold as the masculine as a basis from which to live. Neither man nor woman can create without awareness of and respect for the opposite sex or values.

What is true is that our world depends on finding the feminine values in men and women which have been so terribly neglected over hundreds of years. Instead, many women have gone off into masculine power seeking and have almost a hostile attitude toward men.

ANIMA   But what about those women whose interests and talents lie clearly outside those areas that have traditionally been the domain of women?

H . L .   It's not that I don't admire very greatly many women who have lived public lives. If that is their job in life, then that's beautiful. But the really good ones do it from their feminine wisdom of relatedness and caring. There is no reason a woman can't do any job a man does, provided it's physically possible for her. But she does it as a woman, with a woman's values, or she fails.

ANIMA What are these women's values or feminine values? How do these values manifest themselves in our daily living?

H.L. I think it comes from an innate courtesy toward everything in life—things, animals, people. A basic kindness even. The Dalai Lama once answered a question about what his religion was. And he said, "My religion is only kindness." It is a beautiful word because it means being kin with everything—a sense of the unity behind every manifestation of life.

I have experienced this sense of relatedness in my extreme old age when I occasionally speak to a big group. I can't write anything beforehand, so I just talk spontaneously about something to which I have responded with delight. When I am speaking it is as if I am sharing with each individual in the group. It isn't a willed thing, it just comes naturally.

ANIMA As you were talking I was thinking that this relatedness and respect is very important among women. The women's movement has sent very confusing messages to those who have chosen the traditional roles of wife and mother.

H.L. After all, there still are women who want to stay at home and take care of their children. And they feel inferior because they are doing that. That is also what I mean by the contempt that has gotten into the collective thinking.

ANIMA I had an experience when I was expecting my first child. I was working at a college for women and I went to the president—who was a woman—to discuss the possibility of part-time work after my baby was born. Her reaction to my request was, "Well, I don't think you've decided yet whether you want to be a librarian or a mother." I was so infuriated at the suggestion that I had to choose.

Traditionally, men have not had to make these kinds of choices. The clarity of their roles does look appealing to some women. What are some of the other issues that led women to imitate the masculine rather than find their own way?

H.L. Well, I think it was that women were never given equal rights. That fight was certainly right and still is—where we are not given equal opportunity and such things. On that level, yes. But when it goes to the level that says "We have been so ill treated by men," it is apt to turn negative. There had to be, historically, a long period when the masculine took the lead.

ANIMA What do you mean?

H.L. Without this period, we would have stayed a matriarchy and refused to learn to discriminate. The period in ancient Greece when Athens broke down with corruption was an era very much like our own. At that time, it was the thinking mind that had needed development. Otherwise the feminine mind would have remained in the unconscious. Socrates insisted on the utmost clarity of thought but he knew that his *daimon* was feminine and for this he died, without bitterness against his enemies, talking to his friends.

ANIMA Perhaps it is time to understand our history lessons in a new way. For instance, you can rail against the patriarchy and monotheism, but if it had not occurred we would not have been able to define the next step that takes us beyond it.

H.L. Exactly. You know that takes us back to a basic statement from Jung that I happened to come across again recently. You shouldn't fight a neurosis in order to get rid of it. It is probably the one thing that is necessary for you to learn what is the matter. It is, therefore, the gift of God. It forces you to look at why you are in this neurosis—which will probably turn out to be because you are demanding that life ought to give you what the ego wants in order to feel good.

ANIMA   Every experience gives us feedback. We can either ignore it and go on in our miserable way or we can look at it and learn from it.

Another unfortunate aspect of holding up the masculine and trying to imitate it is that we have not convinced men that there is value in the feminine for their own lives. Instead, we've reinforced their understanding that what they are doing is right.

H.L.   All men need to learn this—some of them have. You often meet in men a kind of tenderness. I was so impressed when I was reading St. John of the Cross and St. Teresa. She is the austere one. He has a wonderful tenderness that you find in a man who does value the feminine.

ANIMA   Can you define more clearly what you mean when you use the word "austere"?

H.L.   A woman, I feel, must always have a certain austerity in her love. She must have a knowledge of when to say no. This austerity can act as a kind of protection from the unconscious tendency of the woman to get caught in love's possessiveness—to become the devouring mother. In any relationship, one or the other, or both at once, can try to eat up the other. Woman, therefore, must have a discipline. She needs to develop her masculine side. I call it her inner spirit of clear discrimination which gives form to her feminine creativity. One of the greatest of feminine creative gifts lies in the depths of her responsiveness to people, to ideas, to life itself. Artists of all kinds have known that until there is response to their work, it does not fully live.

ANIMA   As a wife and the mother of two sons I know how easy it is to slip into the habit of defining yourself in terms of these roles. They can demand so much of your time and energy. It does take great discipline to preserve your sense of individuality and to leave some space between yourself and those whom you love so deeply.

H.L.   Indeed, yes. It is also the essential discrimination between different values in oneself and in the world, just as there is in any relationship between two people. You've got to know who you are and the other person has to know who he or she is before you can really unite. It was Emerson who said you cannot really be a true friend unless you are able to do without your friend. So there has to be, on the level of time and space, separation and the ability to say no when it is against one's emotional desire to do so, before one can even intuit the oneness of the two opposites.

The feminine danger is in wanting to have a big soup. It's true that in the unconscious everything flows into everything else because of the oneness that is at the root of all being. But it seems to me that an essential point of our life in time—in the creation of time and space—is to discriminate. Modern scientists have to discriminate between the tiniest particles. Reality seems to speak in smaller and smaller terms before its meaning is found, but each has to be distinct.

Thoughts and feelings come from two opposites, the heart and the head. It is a marriage between the heart and the head that we have to come to in order to be androgynous. You can call it, using another language, the holy marriage within of the masculine and the feminine, and of the two great principles, the light and the dark. But unless you have experienced them separately first, you can't know the real unity.

ANIMA   I appreciated your comments about the importance of confronting the darkness in *Kaleidoscope*. They are particularly helpful in our time when so many Christian influences keep telling us that the darkness is to be avoided.

H.L.   That is what has bedeviled the churches for hundreds of years. They often teach that there ought not to be any darkness. Well, you wouldn't see any light if there weren't darkness. The light and the shadow are what make the beauty of anything. But if you take away one or the other there is just a sort of uniformity—it's not a union.

Renee Weber has written a book called *Dialogue With Scientists and Sages* which bears on the issue of darkness. She is a professor of philosophy who has known and talked with great scientists and sages from different religions. The Christian sage she interviewed for her book was Father Bede Griffith.

Well, Renee Weber points out in her introduction that only Father Bede stressed the darkness. All the others were talking about the light. And I just think it's interesting. When we live in a world that is full of the kind of darkness we have now there's only one hope and that is to go into it and through it and, in our small way, never try to evade our own little bit of darkness but suffer it consciously.

ANIMA   An English professor at college once told our class about how he dealt with the death of a close friend. He said he went home and played a recording of the saddest music he knew. He plunged into the darkness; he acknowledged his grief and allowed it to pour out. He knew that the only way he could get beyond his loss was to allow himself to feel the pain in all its intensity. In the same way, if we evade the darkness in our lives, we deny some of the most significant portions of our personal and collective experiences.

H.L.   Do you know the *Encyclopedia of Archetypal Symbolism?* It has some wonderful things in it. There's one picture of the crucifixion and, in the commentary that accompanies the picture, the editor has included a letter that Jung wrote to a woman friend. In this letter Jung talks about darkness very clearly as he does so many times. But I thought this was especially beautiful. He said, "There is a mystical fool in me who goes beyond all science." And he went on to say that because of this he had suffered deeply and had known great darkness. But always in the midst of the darkness there was a shining light. And he ends by saying, "Somewhere there seems to be great kindness in the abysmal darkness of the Deity." As I have already said, the word "kindness" is so deep because it means, for me, kinship with every person, every animal, every plant—the entire creation. Everything is kin.

Jung said that it was because of this mystical fool that he was saved from petrification. In the midst of all the science he remained a human being. I think this petrification or hardness of heart is what threatens some of those who simply pour out words. They are often very fine words but they don't live because you don't feel the human being in them. Don't you agree that this is frequent nowadays in people who write about spiritual things?

ANIMA   Perhaps this is because people are striving for control through spirituality.

H.L.   That's right. Or trying to achieve something. One of Meister Eckhart's sayings is that you are never poor in spirit until you stop trying to know God. Which is absolutely true. As long as you are *trying* to have a spiritual experience, it's just a possessive thing and it isn't real.

The new subtitle that they put on the present printing of *Old Age* is "Journey into Simplicity." You have to give up all your goals—especially spiritual goals. It's not easy.

ANIMA   Those of us who have been influenced by patriarchal monotheism have come to accept its orientation toward achievement—its pointer toward the future and its heavenly goal. But as I read about your life and your journey, which has been described as an "ever shifting, extremely individual journey," I have a sense of something circular or spiral.

H.L.   That's the great thing you find out as you grow old. In the middle years when you are busy with your outer work and bringing up a family and all the rest, you still need to know this. But when you are older, it becomes vital. Then you may recognize it as a natural thing.

You know that as we grow older we start remembering old things much more clearly than what happened yesterday. In fact one has trouble remembering yesterday. It can just be nostalgia, without meaning, and it often is. Or it can be a refinding of the whole pattern of your life as a circle or a spiral—that's a beautiful image you have brought. The spiral goes into the dark, into the light, into the dark, into the light. It goes up or down. It goes around. It is the image of the life of the spiritual in humans. But people talk about spirituality so much that it has almost become a cliché.

When I think of the life of the spirit, the image that has the deepest kind of meaning is the tree that goes down as much as it goes up. Without going down, it won't go up. Without going up, it won't go down. It's a beautiful symbol to me.

ANIMA   The other aspect of your journey is that it has been "extremely individual." So much of the work that needs to be done in the world comes down to individual work.

H.L.   That, of course, is Jung's great point. The huge problem for most people on the journey is learning to discriminate between the ego and the Self. You see, most psychological work is based entirely on the ego. It is goal oriented. You've got to become well adjusted. You've got to get rid of all the mistakes and the darkness in your life. You've got to get better from the neurosis. Don't let it teach you, but teach it to go away.

Jung's way is just the opposite. He is not seeking to make you well adjusted to this world. That will happen in the way that is right for you as an individual if you will follow your own truth. And if you go deep enough, it will probably get you into trouble with those who don't understand what the difference is between the ego and the Self.

The trouble with much of this business of trying for spiritual experiences is that it simply reflects an ego that wants to feel good—which isn't the point at all. Your Self is something quite different. Your Self is the only place where you can find peace. It is that which is beyond all your ego's wants and desires and comforts and sufferings. This doesn't mean that they are done away with. You still suffer these things in the ego world and you need to. You still enjoy the happy things with delight. You can't live consciously in time without a good ego, a strong ego. But you have to know what God's intentions—if we're using the word "God"—

are for you. This is what matters, what enables you to find who you are ultimately in this world and why you are here. That is what Jung called "individuation"—your unique completeness.

ANIMA As you talk about the process of discriminating between the ego and the Self, you also acknowledge the importance of making space in our lives for silence. If ever there was an age of chatter it is ours. What happens to us when we have too much noise?

H.L. It gets into the unconscious and keeps your thoughts going chatter, chatter, chatter. You then lose touch with the center of your being and are caught with all kind of worries about unimportant things. Constant worry which hides the *essential* things.

We suffer from this noise—talk, talk, talk. In Victorian times everything was covered over thickly with whitewash and often an undercoat of hypocrisy. Now we have reacted by wanting to talk about everything in public, even the deepest, most secret things. Today, it is vitally important to know that the silence when one is alone is the only place where the final, really transforming thing may be known. But this cannot happen unless you are also in relationship with other people and are having a dialogue. You have to talk with somebody. You need another mind to make known your own. But you also have to know the times and places where you must stay alone. One of Jung's remarks I saw quoted that speaks to this well is, "It takes so much silence to make up for the futility of words."

ANIMA You have seen so much—a century's worth. Your inner journey has uncovered a great deal of wisdom. What are your hopes as you look ahead?

H.L. That is a difficult question. I think my answer would be as T. S. Eliot puts it in his "Four Quartets." "Hope would be hope for the wrong thing." Seers do not hope anymore on the level of cause and effect. What is happening at this moment becomes more and more the only thing they are concerned with.

Do you know of the great theater director Peter Brook? I happened to hear him in an interview on National Public Radio. The question they asked him at the end was, "Which of your great productions would you like to be remembered for?"—a what-do-you-hope-for kind of question. And he said, "That's an honest question. I'll give you an honest answer." And then he said, "I don't know and I don't care, and moreover, it's none of my business." And he went on to explain that he has come more and more to the certainty that all of us must learn to stay in the present moment with all we have.

That's really what Meister Eckhart said. . . . "Wisdom consists in doing the next thing you have to do. Doing it with your whole heart and finding delight in doing it." And that is the simplicity of the feminine values. You stay with the moment, the small thing. You are often made to do this when you get old—you can't do anything else as the old, aging body is apt to teach you!

That wonderful passage in Ecclesiastes, which many people don't read through to the end of, also says it. After the well-known "A time for this and a time for that" it ends with, "That which hath been is now; and that which is to be hath already been; and God requireth that which is past." The future has already been, so what are we worrying about? Every moment has the future contained in it. Well, I think that's the only answer I can give to your question.

ANIMA   That's a good one. It reminds us that tomorrow will take care of itself. Our hopes will not define it.

H . L .   The Self doesn't hope anymore on the levels of cause and effect. The only thing he or she is concerned with is the present moment.

On the other levels of the ego's life it is of the highest importance to hope for a world of increasing recognition, in more and more individuals, of the unity beyond the opposites. This is nourished by every individual who seeks the reality of love beyond personal desire and by the mutual support of *small* groups—groups that remain small—of those who are committed to the journey within and without.

Then the Hope which is expressed by Dante in the Paradiso is born—the Hope which is a certainty of bliss in the heart, however dimly glimpsed. Dante answers St. James in the Paradiso, when he is asked if he has this Hope, by describing it in a metaphor of dew from heaven, which spills from one such heart, overflowing onto others.

LETTING GO

(Note: This interview originally appeared in an issue of *Parabola* magazine, whose theme and title was "Wholeness.")

PARABOLA   You expressed some uneasiness when I told you the theme of this issue and suggested that it might be better if it were called "Approaching Wholeness." Why is that?

HELEN LUKE   I think my feeling is that very few people in any generation do actually come to what we could call wholeness incarnate. There may be a lot more who do so just before they die. But as long as we are in linear time, it cannot be put into words, or talked about really by anyone who is still on the way. There are moments for all of us, I think, when we break out beyond that and have a glimpse of what it is, but the few great ones—those whom the East would call Buddhas, whom we would call those who live the Christ within all the time—are very, very rare. But they do exist. And I do think we should talk about our intuitions of wholeness. This is very important in the beginning. Once one knows it is there, one can be absolutely certain of meaning in life—and go along whatever one's way is, trying to remember. We're so apt to forget.

PARABOLA   It's curious what it is in us which does remember.

H.L. There is something which remembers—it's always there. I don't think anyone who has once experienced it would ever forget entirely. Although it can turn negative.

PARABOLA In what way?

H.L. When it's swallowed up by a power drive from the ego.

PARABOLA The glimpse itself can become an obstacle?

H.L. Well, wholeness must include everything. It is our choice as human beings as to whether we experience it positively or negatively. You may have read Charles Williams's *Descent into Hell*. It's so clear there that Wentworth, who ends up in a state of Hell, does so by small choices along the way. He is absorbed *into* wholeness, though he as a unique person no longer exists. After all, Dante made it very clear that Hell is a choice. People who were in his Hell, if offered Heaven, would not and could not choose it.

PARABOLA You have written that people do get what it is that they want. Why do you think it is that so few seem to choose the path toward wholeness—that so many choose peace, perhaps, rather than struggle?

H.L. It could be said, I think, that we all try to choose peace, but that many move further and further away from it by evasion of the struggles and necessary conflicts of the human journey. What the one on the way to hell chooses all the time is peace for himself; rejection of everybody else except his own ego; like Wentworth, he chooses his own images of a lover instead of an actual lover, and so on. The point about peace is that the true peace does not come until one has been through *all* the struggles of the ego, and until one has accepted boundaries and conflict—to the bitter end. That's what the whole Christian story is about. That's what the Cross is.

PARABOLA   Jung has written that what we call consciousness is just a tiny island in the vast and deep sea of the psyche, and that man is a small part of the whole and can never really know it. So we are limited in many ways.

H.L.   Yes, because we are still centered in the ego, you see: I find it very interesting that you are doing this issue on "Wholeness" after your first issue, which was on "The Hero." We all have to experience at first the strengthening of the ego, the development of its ability to discriminate, to make choices, to get into trouble, to get out of it, and so on. And then comes a point when one has to sacrifice the hero. The hero himself has had to make his sacrifices along the way in order to defeat the dragon, to achieve his aim. Now this in Jungian terms would be the journey of the ego getting to know its shadow side—all the parts that have been repressed, both good and bad. It isn't that the shadow is only the dark elements which we think are wicked, because one can also repress one's positive abilities if one does not want to take the responsibility of living them. But there comes a time when the ego relatively knows all it can, has come to terms with its dark sides, can recognize when it is being possessed by projections, and so on. And when that work is largely done—and this, I think, is a very important moment on Jung's way of individuation, as he called it—there comes a time when we must sacrifice the will to achieve, the time when we then have to let go. It's what Lao-tzu says—that when you are pursuing learning you gain something every day, but when you turn to the Tao—which means wholeness, really—then you drop something every day, you let go of something every day. It's a letting go process, and it takes usually many years, letting go by degrees. For instance, if you don't begin to let go of your will to be successful, to achieve in the outer world—or anywhere else, for that matter, the inner world too—you will go on saying that you must get better and better every day, the ego will go on saying it. What begins that process of letting go is when you can really experience the difference between the ego—that little light of consciousness that we have—and the Self, which is the whole Self, the whole sphere and also the center. The Self is a Jungian term, in India it is the Atman, and in the West the

Christ within, the divine wholeness both immanent in every unique human being and at the same time transcendent and universal. If you are still identified with the ego, after you have had a glimpse of the Self, then you may begin to be possessed by a drive for power even if you weren't before. This is how so many cults develop. The leader had a very real vision at one time as a young man, but then he begins to teach it and it becomes identified with his personal ego. Now in each one of us this can easily happen, to some degree.

PARABOLA   In the hero's journey, then, it is necessary to develop the ego very strongly so that there is then something which can let go?

H.L.   Exactly; through the ego's choices the inner vision becomes incarnate. In a recent book by Russell Lockhart, *Words as Eggs,* he asks in the introduction, what are we to do after we have done the absolutely necessary work of coming to terms with the shadow, with the animus and anima, the masculine in a woman, the feminine in a man, the inner figures? We can now recognize them and know when one of them starts playing tricks and so on—what do we do then? It seems that very often psychologists are not clear when the religious side must take over; not in the literal church sense, but in the deepest spiritual sense.

PARABOLA   In all of your work I feel a kind of interdependence between the way of Jung, turning to what is dark, what is hidden, and the Christian way of turning toward the light of Logos. I don't know if you feel this is so.

H.L.   Yes, but when you say the light of Logos, do you mean God? Well, don't call it Logos, because the Self is not just Logos, it is Eros as well, and indeed, the Self is the unity of opposites. It is the truth of Christianity, too, but you rightly say that Christians so often mistake the light of Logos for the whole. Jung pointed out the absolute necessity for the feminine values without which there would be no perception of Self. This is especially true in our time when everything is geared toward achievement. One of the best antidotes to that is to read Lao-tzu, I think:

"When you do nothing, everything is done." And it's true—if you are talking on the right level. But it's mostly not understood. You see, it is so much a matter of levels. Of course cause and effect and all that comes from them operate in our daily lives on that level the whole time. But it cannot really have a meaning—and that's our great danger—unless we recognize that time itself doesn't exist. That's what physicists are now telling us. It is a very exciting thing in our time, modern physics, which is confirming everything that the East has known for thousands of years.

PARABOLA   The fact that something can be true on one level and utterly false on another causes a great deal of confusion, I think. And also the inaccessibility of a level higher than one is on.

H.L.   Yes. The point of the second half of life, then, is to discover that level which makes all the other levels distinct, yet one in the whole. I have seen as I get *really* old that something fascinating begins to happen. It happens, as everybody knows, that you begin to remember early things in your life very vividly—and then you are apt to forget things that happened yesterday because they're not important anymore somehow. My view is that you do remember things that are really vital, but you forget much that isn't. At any rate, you remember the early things. And then there is, so to speak, a choice: you can either let that state, as so many people naturally do, become nostalgia, or even senility, or what can happen is that those memories suddenly acquire an enormously enhanced meaning in the whole of your life. You begin to see your life as a circle instead of as a straight line. That's just one place where you begin to find that level where everything is a circle. But we have to walk on the straight lines, and we have to experience fully the horizontal and the vertical, the earth and the spirit, and the meeting point at the center before that can happen.

PARABOLA   In Castaneda's book, Don Juan called old age the last enemy, and your description of how that last enemy is overcome is quite different from images of fighting against it, denying it—or simply sinking into it. You are saying that it is a time for continuing to grow—a very important kind of new growth.

H.L. That's the vital thing, and you can only do that by letting things go, not by holding on. It comes, in my experience, little by little, in allowing outer responsibilities to drop away at the right times. But more and more—and I think this is most important—it becomes a matter of turning our attention to the smallest things. I can so easily feel that I have to get over washing the dishes or whatever needs doing around the house in order to get down to doing what is really important—to sit down and write, or meditate, or whatever! After you let go the hero who wants to kill the dragon and go out and conquer, the task becomes a matter of full attention to the smallest fact. And you can catch yourself rejecting a fact. Over and over. Whether it is the fact of this table, or the fact of having slipped and fallen, or whatever may happen to you, or the world, or anything else, but also the fact of the chair you are sitting in. The whole either doesn't exist, or it exists in everything. We are forever trying to exclude the ego's failures—to exclude in order to find our peace that way. But to find our peace by including everything dark and light is a very great suffering for the ego, because it has to give up all its will to dominate. The ego doesn't get any weaker; in fact, it probably gets a lot stronger, and the darkness becomes much darker as consciousness becomes greater. But both are facts. And without both, one cannot come near to that level where wholeness can be lived—at least some of the time!

PARABOLA   Gurdjieff said, "The bigger the angel, the bigger the devil."

H.L. Exactly so. Wasn't it Rilke who refused to go to see Freud or to go into analysis because he said that they might take away his devils, but they'd also take away his angels? And that's true, with most analysis. It can happen when analysis is geared to making someone feel good in the world, adjusted and all the rest. That's the great difference in Jung—he's not concerned about whether you are terribly well adjusted in the world, because what he's interested in is the psyche in its relationship to the Self. The ego is terribly important—it's still a complex, it's still there—but it can become one with the Self without losing its uniqueness. That's the marvelous thing.

PARABOLA   I have a question here about how words can mean such different things, for example relationship and dependence, which on the one hand can mean an excuse and an escape—to lose oneself in relationship with another, to escape responsibility in dependence. On the other hand there is true relationship and real dependence arising from the facts you were just speaking of. Related to this is the child who appears to have a kind of wholeness and integrity, and the adult, who seems to have to go through a process of fragmentation and division before the meaning of relationship and dependence can become so utterly different.

H.L.   Yes, that really is the point. The enormous difference is that when you begin to know yourself and to glimpse the Self—the wholeness in which all relationship is free and yet essential—you are no longer relating through projection. The child is simply unconsciously one with the wholeness of everything. As soon as it begins to say "I," then comes the beginning of that kind of dependence which is projection. There is a kind of magical attraction from the unconscious. You are part of an archetypal situation—mother and child, and so on. The work of gaining consciousness is to free yourself from identification with one person or another. If you find you hate a person or that there is something that makes you absolutely furious, you may be perfectly sure that it is a part of yourself that is projected there—no matter how true it may be that the other person is behaving badly. You could see that without getting all het up about it. It's normal that one should be angry at things that go on, but there's quite a different quality in that anger if you have ceased to project. If you are projecting you are incapable of compassion, you are incapable of understanding that this person is behaving in this way for reasons that you cannot see, from problems that you know nothing about, but that we all share.

PARABOLA Just to be sure I'm clear here, projection is really a kind of identification of yourself with the other?

H.L. And you don't do it deliberately. It just happens. Projection is the way you see everything that is unconscious in yourself. If you didn't have that projection, you'd never see it. You wouldn't even know you had it. Once you begin to take projections back, this magical kind of tie changes. Once you begin to let go—and this takes a great deal of hard work and watching, and attention and humility: when once you can ask, "What is it in me that *must* have this to depend on?"—the minute you begin to make that separation between yourself and that projection it may then become a sense of relationship. This is so even if it is a relationship with something you dislike and will go on disliking—no one is trying to tell you that you ought to feel differently in that sense—but it will also be compassionate. That, I believe, is what the East means by saying all is emptiness, all is compassion. Not just emptiness—nothing there—but filled with compassion, which is a suffering with whatever is involved. You see the difference? It doesn't mean you can do without relationship: very much the opposite. But you recognize that relationship cannot happen until you are separate. Otherwise it is just a mixup in the unconscious of two people. You have to separate in order to unite, because uniting means two unique things that meet. Not two fuzzy things—that merge!

That gradual letting go still has to have a context. I think it's enormously important to realize as we work with dreams and the unconscious and other people do the same kind of work in different ways, that when you have an insight it's not enough just to understand. It has then somehow to be put into actual life. It has to be incarnate. This is the true meaning of Christianity. Someone will say he or she has had a big dream and that she feels what it means and so on—she or he must do *something* with it, write it down, paint it, do something *in this world* with it, and after that let it take effect in daily life. It has to make a change, however tiny. This is nearly always a letting go of something. It's all a preparation, of course, for the final letting go of death.

PARABOLA   You have written something about forgiveness that I wanted to ask you about. You wrote, ". . . it is the breakthrough of forgiveness, in its most profound sense—universal and particular, impersonal and personal—that alone brings the 'letting go,' the ultimate freedom of the spirit. For in the moment of that realization every false guilt, whether seen as one's own or as other people's, is gone forever—and the real guilt which each of us carries, of refusal to see, to be aware, is accepted. So we may look open-eyed at ourselves and the world and suffer the pain and joy of the divine conflict which is the human condition, the meaning of incarnation." It seems that something must appear to make this possible, to make one *able*.

H . L .   It may appear in something that happens to you, comes to you from the outer world, or it may appear from something that comes to you suddenly from the inner world. It will happen through a long history of choices in small things. The unwillingness to see is to say no to life, to the risk of mistakes, to facts.

PARABOLA   Do you think that with all the difficulties something helps as well?

H . L .   Oh, but of course! The difficulties are what help most!

PARABOLA   I mean that the right difficulties are brought to you at the right time.

H . L .   I think that if one has faith in the meaning of life at all, that is a certainty.

PARABOLA   It's all arranged?

H.L. I don't like the word "arranged." It just *is*. It's your fate, and you have a choice how to live it. The East would call it your karma.

PARABOLA I have a question about what is really one's own. Certainly all the energies of youth are given, one's talents, weakness, and so on are given, but they all seem like raw material. Is there something at the end which could be there and have the taste of being one's own?

H.L. Your own—how do you mean that? That seems to be a matter of discrimination in the use of words. How does St. Paul put it? "Having nothing, yet possessing all things." Now I would rather have it the other way round, as possessing nothing, yet having all things, because there are so many negative meanings to possession. But it means the same thing, of course. In the ultimate wholeness we surely have everything, but we don't have it exclusively. It isn't ours and not somebody else's. That's the difference, and that is the letting go. You don't any longer feel, "I have the right to this." You don't have rights, you don't have demands, you don't have wishes. No, that's not true, your ego has them all the time! Don't think you are going to lose your ego's carryings-on; you're not. You merely are not moved by them in the old way. Less and less are they the center of your life. They operate on a certain level, but they become less and less demanding—of people, of things, of everything. Meister Eckhart said we must let go even of the demand to know God. Then it becomes yours. Then it is given to you—when it is completely let go.

PARABOLA Well, there seems to be some sort of task that we have in the course of our lives, and there must be an enormous difference between a person who achieves this aim and one who does not. As we are, this remains only a possibility in us.

H.L. It's a possibility, and it is enormously important for the whole world that some individuals grow to a deep and full consciousness.

PARABOLA Is there something which characterizes the way toward this?

H . L .   I think there is something that one can notice in one's own life very clearly. There comes a point when an utterly different kind of suffering is possible, not a neurotic suffering. At the same time that one begins to move beyond the hero/villain stage, one no longer goes up and down into exaltations and depressions. It is the kind of suffering that comes when you accept the fact of whatever it is—a depression is when you don't accept the fact. The suffering which is not a depression can bring a deeper darkness, but it doesn't affect your behavior or those around you. The weight is gone, because there will also be a kind of joy that goes with it, which is nothing emotional. There is a possibility to move beyond being dominated by your emotions. That's the mistake people always make—we think we always have to be improving the ego. We don't. We have to put it through its journey of knowing itself and understanding itself, and so on, and then we shall recognize that its emotions are not objective. They are purely subjective, which is a necessary stage. But then comes what Jung calls objective cognition, and the kind of love he writes about in his autobiography, *Memories, Dreams, Reflections*. The love that is beyond all desiring, all emotions; and that is whole in itself because nothing is excluded.

PARABOLA   Feeling without emotion?

H . L .   None of these words somehow express it because it is a state of being, a state of the soul. In fact it is reality itself. But one just glimpses these things, now and then.

PARABOLA   It is a long way from the way compassion is sometimes understood—as a sea of emotionality.

H . L .   The feeling of wishing to save the world comes very often out of a wish to escape from having compassion on your own darkness, for what is inside yourself. If you don't start there you will never have true compassion. First comes compassion for your own weaknesses, and then for the person next to you. Now that doesn't mean that we shouldn't support causes—what matters is *who* supports the causes. You may have to fight, but if you don't fight with forgiveness and compassion, you simply are recreating the same situation. One opposite always creates the other, unless you begin to let go of both of them, then both can become real in a unity which is beyond them.

PARABOLA   What you say brings to mind the words of Dame Julian of Norwich which you've written about. "All shall be well by the purification of the motive in the ground of our beseeching."

H.L.   That's really the point, isn't it, "by the purification of the motive . . ."? Actually this quotation is from T. S. Eliot's "Four Quartets." The motive—that which moves us from the very ground of our being—is slowly purified here in time through the individual's commitment to the emptying process which is the quest of wholeness. Then, in Lady Julian's words, "All shall be well, and all manner of thing shall be well."

GLOSSARY

ANIMA AND ANIMUS: Personifications of the unconscious femininity in the psyche of man and of the unconscious masculinity in the psyche of woman. In her negative form the anima will manifest herself in a man's irrational moods and emotions; the negative animus is made up of a woman's secondhand opinions, sweeping generalizations, and imperatives. Their positive natural function, once we relate to them, is to act as guides to the unconscious and to the creative images within.

ARCHETYPE: The archetypes themselves are the indefinable natural forces underlying human life in all ages and all places. They cannot be known directly, but archetypal themes appear all over the world in myth, in fairy tales, fantasies, dreams, etc. We can recognize these archetypal motifs by their fascination, their irrational power to move us. A few of the most frequent archetypal symbols are the hero, the wise old man, the nourishing and devouring mother, the water of life, and so on.

CONSCIOUSNESS AND THE UNCONSCIOUS: The conscious mind contains all that we know, and the ego is the carrier of this knowledge. The unconscious comprises all that we do not know in the inner world, from personal repressions to all the vast possibilities of the psyche, future, and past.

EGO: "The conscious thinking subject" (Oxford English Dictionary).

EROS: The Greek god of love. Psychologically, Eros is the love that brings healing and balance to the split in the psyche, but may also, if so *used* by the soul, degenerate into lust.

EXTRAVERSION: A psychic attitude characterized by a concentration of interest in objects; easily susceptible to outer influences, it often brings denial of the reality of inner, irrational values.

HIEROSGAMOS: Sacred marriage, union of opposites.

HUBRIS: The Greek word for overweening pride which seeks to usurp the power of the gods. It led to *nemesis*, the vengeance of the gods.

INTROVERSION: A concentration on inner psychic processes, oriented to an inner evaluation of experience. If extreme, it may lead to an undervaluation of outer reality.

LOGOS: The creative word of God; conscious masculinity, the seed of life.

MANA: A Melanesian word for a supernatural power felt in a person, event, or object.

MANDALA: A "magic" circle, symbolizing psychic totality and expressing the pattern of life around the center. Mandalas are found all over the world. They were used especially in India as "yantras"—aids to contemplation. Their structure is usually based on the number four within the circle. Their forms are often variations on the flower, the cross, or the wheel. Traditional mandalas, whether Eastern or Christian, have the Deity at the center. Individuals nowadays often produce mandalas spontaneously from the unconscious, and the center is apt to be a point. They are not consciously contrived patterns.

METANDIA: Transformation of spirit.

NUMINOUS: An adjective which describes that wonder which is felt by an individual who is moved by or transformed by a symbol (q.v.); a mystery transcending rational thought or analysis.

PROJECTION: Everything of which we are unconscious is "projected" into the outer world, and we see it in events and people outside ourselves. Thus the less conscious we are of our own rejected and inferior qualities and of the realities of the inner world, the less objectivity we have in our judgments of people and things, for they are hidden behind our projections of our unknown selves.

PSYCHE: The psyche is defined in the dictionary as soul, spirit, mind. As used by Jung, it includes all the nonphysical realities of the human being.

SELF: Jung has used this term to express the idea of the center—the center which is also the circumference—the totality of the personality, embracing all, both consciousness and the unconscious. This center of being has a thousand names: the Atman in India, Christ in Christianity, the stone in alchemy, the diamond, the child, the flower, the circle, the square, the Tao in China. All these are but a few of the symbols through which men have experienced this central mystery of life.

SHADOW: The shadow (in dreams always of the same sex as the dreamer) personifies all the inferior and rejected sides of the personality. These shadow qualities are not all negative, but may also be potentialities for which the ego has not taken responsibility.

SYMBOL: The meeting point of conscious and unconscious meanings which awaken in us an awareness of something that cannot be expressed in rational terms.

CPSIA information can be obtained at www.ICGtesting.com
Printed in the USA
LVOW11s1836210615

443297LV00001B/217/P